ABERDEEN
IN THE
NINETEENTH CENTURY

Aberdeen in the Nineteenth Century

The Making of the Modern City

edited by

JOHN S. SMITH and DAVID STEVENSON

ABERDEEN UNIVERSITY PRESS

First published 1988
Aberdeen University Press
A member of the Pergamon Group

© Centre for Scottish Studies, University of Aberdeen 1988

British Library Cataloguing in Publication Data

Aberdeen in the nineteenth century: the
    making of the modern city.—(Aberdeen
    University Centre for Scottish Studies
    series on local history).
    1. Scotland. Grampian Region. Aberdeen,
    1837-1901
    I. Smith, John S. II. Stevenson, David
    III. Series
    941.2′35081

ISBN 0 08 036575 2

PRINTED IN GREAT BRITAIN
THE UNIVERSITY PRESS
ABERDEEN

CONTENTS

ILLUSTRATIONS

PREFACE

With *New Light on Medieval Aberdeen* (1985) the Centre for Scottish Studies presented the results of recent research on the town in the Middle Ages. In *Lairds and Louns. Country and Burgh Life in Aberdeen, 1600-1800* (1986) the focus widened to include the shire as well as the town in the Early Modern period. Now, in the third collection of papers from the Centre's popular series of local history conferences, the focus narrows again to the burgh, and examines it in the great age of development that did so much to define the layout and appearance of its central area right up to the present. The nineteenth century did indeed see *The Making of the Modern City*, the subtitle we have given this book, but equally appropriate would have been *The Great Age of Granite*, for it is the work of nineteenth century architects and stonemasons with that intractable stone which gives central Aberdeen its unique identity among British cities, a distinctiveness immediately evident to even the most casual of visitors. Not until their work was done could Aberdeen boast to be 'The Granite City' or even (when wishing to soften the hard image evoked by that phrase) 'The Silver City'.

Gratitude is due to the authors of the papers for making them available for publication in this series of Aberdeen University Press occasional studies sponsored by the Centre. The work of Rod Gunson, the Centre's Conference Organiser, ensured that the conference on 31 October 1987 at which the papers were originally delivered was a most successful day, and a notable contribution was also made by John Smith, the Centre's pamphlet editor, who chaired the meeting with the necessary mixture of tact and firmness.

DAVID STEVENSON
Director of the Centre for Scottish Studies
and Reader in Scottish History,
University of Aberdeen

ABERDEEN—THE GREAT CENTURY

R.E.H. Mellor

Just twelve years from the end of our own century we may look back and compare its impact on Aberdeen with that of the nineteenth century. Perhaps in the millenium that our century brings to an end the nineteenth century was the most momentous in the city's thousand year history. Let us review the evidence for calling it 'the great century'.

Of course we must recognise that Aberdeen's development has been powerfully influenced by the broader trends that from time to time have swept across Europe. It was in the upsurge in urban life and commerce spreading across Europe in the twelfth century that real take-off occurred in our burgh. Subsequent growth and development was slow, sometimes halted by war, political crises or natural disasters, most notably plagues. From the evidence available, particularly James Gordon's map and description, we can recognise many features of the modern town by the late seventeenth century. It was, however, the eighteenth century that laid the basis from which expansion in the following century was to blossom. The early eighteenth century saw the gradually widening horizons of commerce as the mercantilist imperium of the English was opened to the Scots by the Act of Union of 1707, but it was the scientific and technological advances from the middle of the century that fired the immense social and economic change of the 'Industrial Revolution'. It is also important to remember that the much acclaimed industrial revolution was paralleled by an agrarian revolution whose impact for the burgh was to be little less significant. The industrialisation of Britain and the associated growth of commerce favoured towns as agglomerative growth poles, an influence Aberdeen could not escape. By the 1770s

Aberdeen was already a thrusting and bustling place of accelerating change.

As the Hogmanay bells rang in the year 1800, no magic transformation took place, but the foundation of ongoing and increasingly rapid change soon became apparent, the hallmark of the new century. The century may be divided into three roughly equal parts, each with a distinct keynote in development. The first, lasting to around 1830, witnessed great effort to improve accessibility to and mobility in the inner town by laying out new streets. It also saw modest improvements in public health provision, a process begun in the mid-eighteenth century throughout Britain, where better public hygiene was a significant contributory factor in the population 'explosion' of the industrial revolution. The second period, ending in the 1860s, had as its keynote the coming to fruition of work to improve the harbour. There also took place the revolution in transport brought by the railway, vital in providing ease of movement for trade in an expanding economic horizon. The third period, which we may see running on until 1914, was one of the further steady improvement in the quality of life, with considerable suburban expansion made possible by municipal transport provision. Health and educational provision, in keeping with legislation at national level, were also bettered. It was a time of considerable prosperity and wealth creation. Of course, such keynote developments of any one period had often begun to stir in the preceding one and usually continued into those succeeding it.

The later eighteenth century saw accelerating growth in the burgh and by the end of the century an extension to the boundaries was imperative. Even more pressing, however, was creation of easier access into the town as wheeled traffic rose as turnpikes were built following the Turnpike Act of 1795. The narrow, twisting and often steep streets and alleys amid the rough terrain were unable to cope with the volume of traffic passing over them as population and commerce expanded. To ease movement, clear thoroughfares into the heart of the town were needed, and they would also improve access to land around the town suitable for development. In a burgh of hardly 30,000 people but rapidly growing, a bold and imaginative plan to build new streets was pursued. Though it briefly brought the burgh to bankruptcy (1817), the economic buoyancy of the post-Napoleonic period was sufficient to facilitate recovery within eight years.

The central project in this plan gave the modern city its aorta—Union Street. Even by modern civil engineering standards, the work required massive effort and is quite staggering when seen in terms of navvies, wheelbarrows and horse carts. The northern flank of St Katherine's Hill had to be levelled and a line of arches built to carry the new street (crossing over several of the medieval streets), the most daunting of all being the 130 foot span of the majestic Union Bridge, sadly now partly concealed by unsympathetic modern development (plates 1-4). Construction of the new street also meant purchasing and clearing much old and crowded property. At its western end Union Street divided, one continuation (into Albyn Place) leaving us a masterpiece of the early nineteenth-century developer's skill, while the other, the exit to the south, was well laid out but undistinguished.

The other major new street, King Street, was constructionally much less challenging, providing a fine straight exit to the north. It did not become fully effective, however, until linked to the Ellon turnpike on completion of Telford's splendid Bridge of Don (1830). A third new street, alas very undistinguished, George Street, gave access to the Inverurie turnpike, but it faced crossing wet ground over the remains of the old loch. It is interesting that each of these new thoroughfares paralleled one of the old traditional routes out of town. Almost each year through this first period a new street or streets appeared on the burgh map.

The second achievement of this time was creation of the image of the Granite City. Aberdeen in early times had been a town largely of wood and thatch, alarmingly prone to fire, but further such building was banned in 1731, by which time most houses were constructed in crudely fashioned stone, often river or glacial boulders, but increasingly augmented by quarried stone and better masonry. The almost exclusive use of cut granite came as local firms developed ever greater skill in cutting and polishing the stone during the 1820s and 1830s. The popularity of granite increased as it became so attractively displayed by the gifted architecture of Archibald Simpson and

1. Union Bridge under construction. (Original in possession of University of Aberdeen).

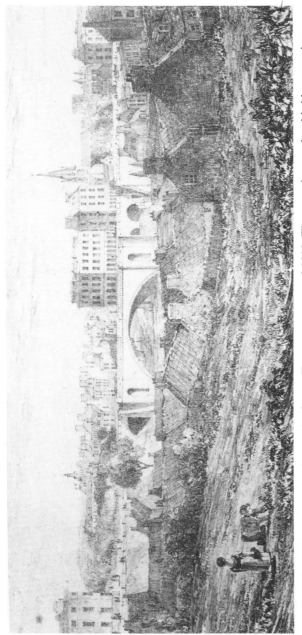

2. Union Bridge from what is now the Crown Terrace area around 1810. The recently completed bridge spanning the Den Burn valley contrasts with the pantiled cottages in the right foreground which occupy the slope running down Bridge Street (1865-7). The very considerable engineering works associated with the construction of Union Street are perhaps best appreciated by contrasting the older buildings on the Green with the newly constructed block between Belmont Street and the bridge, originally the *Aberdeen Hotel*. (Original in possession of University of Aberdeen).

3. The Den Burn valley looking southwards towards the Bow Brig and the Green. At the time this view was sketched (1807), the newly completed bridge lay on the edge of the countryside. (Original in possession of University of Aberdeen).

4. Mutton Brae, the Den Burn and Hadden's Mill in the Green. The pantiled cottages in the left foreground were occupied by handloom weavers who in the early nineteenth century chiefly worked in the cotton factory of Gordon, Barron and Co. sited until 1830 at the corner of Belmont Street and Schoolhill. The site of the factory was subsequently utilised for the construction of Archibald Simpson's three Free Churches nestling under the prominent brick spire. The cottages were to be swept away during the construction of the Denburn Valley Junction Railway and the last disappeared with the completion of the Schoolhill Viaduct in 1899.

John Smith. The full effect is well seen in many Union Street buildings of the time (plates 5-6) and in the elegant squares and streets on either side of this main thoroughfare, and also in King Street and in Ferryhill. Perfecting the art of granite working continued through the century, culminating in such elaborately fashioned facades as Marischal College (rebuilding begun 1891), and the unusual dwelling house at 50 Queen's Road (1886) or the Atholl Hotel (1860) in King's Gate.

Early nineteenth-century Britain witnessed a growing concern with public health and Aberdeen kept more than pace in this development. Memories lingered of grim seventeenth-century plagues and there was a real fear of cholera, brought to Britain from the Baltic in 1831. The first real improvement dated back to 1742, with the opening of the first infirmary at Woolmanhill, which within eight years needed extension and which in 1773 had received a royal charter. Additional accommodation was created in 1818 and 1833, while an entirely new building was erected on the site in 1840, but it was still to be further enlarged and extended in 1887. A separate mental hospital was opened at Cornhill, extended in 1819 and again in 1860. In 1803 a Vaccine Institution had been established, while somewhat earlier a dispensary had been founded, subsequently supplemented by a further two. The opening of a Lying-in Institution in 1823 provided a forerunner of the Maternity Hospital. By 1843, the Blind Asylum had been opened, while later Victorian additions were the City Hospital (long regarded as the 'fever hospital') and the Sick Children's Hospital in Castle Terrace.

Proof in 1854 that contaminated water was a key factor in the spread of cholera gave new importance to adequate clean water supplies. Some improvements had been made in early-eighteenth century Aberdeen but rapidly proved inadequate and through the nineteenth century, even until our own day, constant augmentation has been necessary as population grew and individual consumption rose. By the 1790s increasing the supply had become a problem as all immediate sources in the town had been exploited. A dry summer in 1826 raised the issue to crisis proportions, so in 1829 the Dee near the Bridge of Dee was tapped, but by 1855 further supplies were again needed. In 1864 there began a flow from Cairnton further upstream,

5. Union Street in the 1880s with the horse trams plying their trade. (Macbean Collection, University of Aberdeen).

6. Late nineteenth century Union Street when pedestrians ruled supreme. (Macbean Collection, University of Aberdeen).

some nineteen miles away, a source which was to have its capacity enlarged several times. By this time the old 'fountains' for public supply were being phased out as water was delivered by pipe into individual dwellings. An act of 1862 empowered the council to make all house-owners pipe in water for a sink and water closet wherever there was a water pipe within ten yards of the property.

The burgh continued to grow and population had risen from 26,900 in 1801 to 73,805 by 1861 and more streets and houses had had to be added to accommodate the people and their activities. The keynote of the second period lay, however, in improvement in transport. Certainly the turnpikes had done much to ease movement, but really long distance transport still relied principally upon the sea, especially for freight. The Dee estuary had always provided something of a natural harbour, but growth in the size and number of vessels using the port focused attention on the need for better anchorage, easier access across the bar and adequate quays. Some simple works had already been carried out but much more was required to be done. Substantial improvement had come with Smeaton's north pier of 1788, even if it had not been carried out as he intended, while in 1797 Rennie pointed the way for further improving works. A third doyen of British civil engineering became involved when in 1801 Telford had been appointed consultant. For thirty years some of the most crucial of all improvement work went on under his direction. The details of these improvements are discussed in a separate essay, but suffice it to say that each improvement increased the port's capacity and its prosperity. Such work was to continue right through the century, considerably strengthened by the Harbour Act of 1868 that founded the Harbour Board of Management. The success of the port is indicated by the way it flourished despite the coming of the railway that spelled decline for many once prosperous ports. Hand in hand with these developments went shipbuilding that enjoyed its greatest repute between 1839 and 1869. These were the years when Aberdeen's yards turned out splendid clipper ships, most famous of which was *Thermopylae*. Thereafter the industry continued successfully but building more prosaic steamships and iron vessels.

The opening of the Liverpool and Manchester Railway in

1830 signalled one of the most revolutionary events of the whole industrial revolution. The railways' impact on mobility was immense and they quickly displaced stage coaches and canals. The Aberdeenshire Canal, opened in 1807 from the harbour to Port Elphinstone, was to be a victim when its bed was used for the Kittybrewster to Huntly railway, opened in 1854, the core of the later distinctive regional company for the North East of Scotland, the Great North of Scotland Railway. By 1858 through traffic to Inverness was possible, and most important places in Buchan and Banffshire were linked by rail to Aberdeen in the 1860s and 1870s. The first appearance of the railway in the burgh had, however, come from the south in 1850, a vital link to southern markets actively supported by Aberdeen merchants from as early as 1844. It proved a quick and reliable outlet for fish, cattle and other local produce to growing markets elsewhere in Scotland and beyond, a serious competitor for the port of Aberdeen. Surprisingly, the two railways were not linked until completion of the Denburn Valley line in 1867. The burgh was, however, put on the map in the Railway Age when Aberdeen became the destination for 'races' between rival companies from London. The London North-Western Railway and the Caledonian Railway along the west coast route ultimately triumphed over the Great Northern Railway, the North-Eastern Railway and the North British Railway along the east coast route during much advertised runs in 1888 and 1895.

The 1860s determined in the third period much of the outline and infrastructure of the burgh which was to last until the metamorphosis of the Oil Boom a century later. Things far from stood still and the rate of change was probably as hard to stomach for Aberdonians of the day as the Oil Boom has been for those of today. Continuing growth meant the burgh was again beginning to burst at the seams and the outcome was boundary extensions: in 1871 these were mostly on the south around the estuary, and other additions came in 1883. A massive extension in 1891 more than doubled the burgh's area, incorporating the then independent burghs of Old Aberdeen and Woodside and swallowing the burgeoning settlement of Torry. In the 1870s population rose above the magic 100,000 mark to add another major city to the map of Europe.

This was a time when many public and commercial buildings

still in use were erected, sweeping away most surviving remnants of the early town, as when the new Town House was built in 1867. New wealth encouraged commercial development, with a readiness to demolish some fine but neglected properties of seventeenth-century or earlier origin. Bent on progress, Victorians showed little reverence for monuments of the past, sadly setting a trend long pursued in the burgh. Much clearance of crowded and insanitary property, once fine town houses, was done in the name of public health, but thought of refurbishment (as carried out in recent years) never seemed to be entertained in those days. A major development came as Torry grew rapidly from the 1880s onwards as fishing gained a new impetus. Originally accessible circuitously by the 'Chain Bridge' (1830), its closer integration came on completion of a more direct approach along Market Street and the Victoria Bridge (1881), a welcome addition after the Torry ferry disaster of 1876, one of the blackest days of Victorian Aberdeen. Another major development, characteristically bold, was completion in 1883 of Rosemount Viaduct, easing access to the north west of the town, surmounting in monumental fashion another of the old constraints on growth imposed by the rough terrain (plate 17).

The wealth of Victorian Britain is epitomised in the suburbs of the time, the massive granite family houses along Queen's Road, Great Western Road, King's Gate and in the Rubislaw district among others. Even the less affluent were housed in solid and often stately tenement blocks, as in Rosemount and Union Grove, a considerable contrast to the redbrick 'Coronation Street' terraces of English industrial towns. The suburban spread was given additional momentum by the coming of the tram, first horse-drawn (1872) and later (1899) electrically powered. There was also general improvement in urban amenity, exemplified by public parks like the Victoria Park (1871), Union Terrace Gardens (1872) and Duthie Park (1883). Though gas had been available from 1824, it did not become widespread in use until later, even though a second supply company had been established in 1843, and the real upsurge came after 1871 when gas supply was taken over by the corporation. Electricity was first supplied only in 1894, but the first public supply in Britain had not been available until 1881. Discovery of the relationships between the spread of disease, waste disposal and contamination of water in mid-century was quickly followed by most major towns improving their system of sewage disposal, and Aberdeen was not left behind as work began about 1866 and was speeded up when the council was made responsible in 1871.

Aberdonians were no exception to the Victorian awareness of the importance of education, perhaps doing more than many comparable towns. They started with some advantage, a university in the burgh and another nearby in the 'Old Town', to be united in 1860 though both campuses remained in use. Early in the century, school places were hardly adequate for all the children in the burgh, though the existing schools were of considerable repute. In addition to Robert Gordon's College of 1750, several private schools were established during Victoria's reign (notably St Margaret's 1846, Albyn 1867 and the Convent School 1897), but public education received a great stimulus from the Education Act of 1872. Subsequent to this Act, numerous schools still in use today were built and two training colleges for teachers under church auspices opened in 1873 and 1875 (eventually merged in 1906). Robert Gordon's College also developed under the act's aegis a Technical College, though a Mechanics' Institute had existed as early as 1824. In 1883 Gray's School of Art appeared, followed a year later by the Art Gallery.

Mid-century the economic situation of Aberdeen had been a little uncertain, but by the later part the industrial structure had taken much of the character it was to retain until the Oil Boom of the 1970s. From its peak early in the century, the textile industry had been overtaken by the great textile districts elsewhere in Britain, but it was to survive into the twentieth century by concentration on quality goods and specialised products. Paper-making arrived in the mid-eighteenth century and was to flourish throughout the nineteenth century, taking advantage after 1864 of esparto grass imported through the port. Around the 1870s there were five mills employing some 2,500 people. Even before 1800 there were engineering shops in the burgh and in the 1870s chemical manufacture was established, both industries—like much else in Aberdeen of the time—geared to agricultural or shipping needs. Most distinctive was the granite industry (now little more than a memory), for in and around the burgh were quarries and near the centre were the yards that polished, cut and sculptured it. There was a successful export trade to London and overseas (even to America).

By the end of the century the burgh's reputation abroad was centred on fishing. Something of the image of Aberdeen as an independent port had passed with the demise of the clipper ships, but during the 1880s a new one as a fishing port quickly emerged. Surprisingly, the town had earlier failed to capitalise on the riches of its adjacent waters, where fishing had been left largely to the Dutch. In the 1870s herring fishers attracted to the port did quite well for themselves and 'Aberdeen herring' became a mark of quality in the Baltic, where the burgh's seaborne commerce had long been active. The arrival in 1882 of the first steam trawler rapidly set a new course—white fish. Success depended considerably on the railway to get the fish speedily to southern markets: fish despatched early one afternoon could be in Billingsgate for the next morning's sale. The wealth brought by this phase was far to outshine that made earlier in the century in granite or in the eighteenth- century linen industry. As the trawlers (mostly built in Aberdeen) brought in more and more wealth, so ancillary industries such as providing ice or processing fish or making boxes flourished. War in 1914 brought an abrupt halt, from which there was never thereafter a proper recovery.

The century ended in a crowning accolade: in 1899 the status of Royal Burgh (since about 1165) was raised to that of the 'County of the City of Aberdeen'.

We see from this brief review of the nineteenth century that Aberdeen was quite transformed and the legacy of that transformation is still with us today, certainly dominating the visual townscape and setting the matrix of much of our daily life. Any Victorian Aberdonian transported by time-machine to the city of today would still feel at home, despite all the scientific and technological advance in the intervening years. No doubt such a time-traveller would find our time less strange than if the transporter had run back, even if only to the late eighteenth century!

Loyal Aberdonians would claim with considerable justification that this vast change was the product of local vision and canny management: certainly the inexplainable human factor lies at the root of all geography. But they must also recognise the broader framework in which such change occurred. It was a time of remarkable peace—wars like those in the Crimea or South Africa did little to alter the course of daily life at home. The early century enjoyed an economic boom in the aftermath of the Napoleonic Wars, a springboard for British economic development that for many formative years made it the 'workshop of the world'. Throughout the period, however, technology was drawing Aberdeen close to the mainstream thought of the world—the railway and the steamship, the telegraph (1854) and the telephone (1881) shrank distance and accelerated the spread of news and ideas. Used to making the best of a modest resource endowment, Aberdonians capitalised on these developments: it is to their credit they did so well in such a bullish and fast changing milieu. Just consider that population in the burgh rose during the nineteenth century by 470% (mostly by in-migration) contrasted to a mere 63% so far this century—and it is highly unlikely the twelve remaining years will see a surge sufficient to compete.

Would Victorian Aberdonians be impressed by our achievements this century? Certainly much of the scientific and technological advance would meet with approval—they would certainly applaud Foresterhill and all its modern medicine and be suitably amazed by the radio and television transmitted from today's city. With a population 100,000 greater than in 1900, there would be obvious surprise at the massive suburban sprawl within the greatly extended boundaries—though they might not be pleased that this development had covered so many of their favourite quiet nooks and picnic spots! They would no doubt applaud the personal mobility brought by the motor car that had made such a spread possible. The high-rise buildings which have so changed the skyline might impress them less. How would they rate the new Conference Centre (so like a giant DIY greenhouse) against the stately classicism of the Music Hall (1820)? One would sympathise if they disliked the new shopping centres for changing the inner city too much and for lacking any hallmark of Aberdeen. They might certainly find the new hotels visually inferior to the sadly defunct Palace Hotel. To tell them there are plans to eradicate The Green might be too much! What would fascinate them most? Perhaps the airport, another artefact in shrinking space, even more dramatically than the railway. Viewed in this manner, we can have little hesitation in claiming the nineteenth century to have been Aberdeen's great century if not a golden age.

BIBLIOGRAPHY

A. Briggs, etc., *The Nineteenth Century— The Contradictions of Progress* (London, 1985).

W.A. Brogden, *Aberdeen—An Illustrated Architectural Guide* (Edinburgh, 1986).

V.E. Clark, *The Port of Aberdeen* (Aberdeen, 1921).

A. Cluer, *Walkin' the Mat* (Aberdeen, 1976).

A. Cluer, *Walkin' the Mat (A second collection)* (Aberdeen, 1984).

N. Cossons, *The BP Book of Industrial Archaeology* (Newton Abbot, 1975).

A. Durie, R.E.H. Mellor (eds.), *George Washington Wilson and Scottish Railways* (Keighley, 1983).

G.M. Fraser, *Aberdeen Street Names* (Aberdeen, 1911).

G.M. Fraser, *The Old Deeside Road* (Aberdeen, 1921).

H. Hamilton, 'Industries and Commerce' in *The North-East of Scotland* (British Association Handbook, Aberdeen, 1963).

A. Keith, *A Thousand Years of Aberdeen* (Aberdeen, 1972).

R.E.H. Mellor (ed.), *The Railways of Scotland—Papers of Andrew C. O'Dell* (Aberdeen, 1984).

R.E.H. Mellor, J.S. Smith, *A Visitor's Guide to Aberdeen* (Aberdeen, 1986).

O.S. Nock, *The Railway Race to the North* (London, 1958).

J. Patrick, *The Coming of Turnpikes to Aberdeenshire* (Aberdeen).

J.C. Rennie, 'Local Government in Scotland' in *The North-East of Scotland* (British Association Handbook, Aberdeen, 1963).

J.S. Smith, 'The Development of Aberdeen Harbour' *Aberdeen University Review* 164 (Aberdeen, 1980).

J.S. Smith, 'The Rise and Fall of Aberdeen's Granite Industry' *Aberdeen University Review* 167 (Aberdeen, 1982).

J.S. Smith, *George Washington Wilson's Aberdeen* (Keighley, 1982).

L.D. Stamp, *Geography of Life and Death* (London, 1965).

J.R. Turner, *Scotland's North Sea Gateway—Aberdeen Harbour 1136-1986* (Aberdeen, 1986).

H.A. Vallance, *The Great North of Scotland Railway* (London, 1965).

J.J. Waterman, *The Coming of the Railway to Aberdeen in the 1840s* (Aberdeen).

J.J. Waterman, *Aberdeen and the Fishing Industry* (Aberdeen).

W.H. Watson, *A. Marshall Mackenzie—Architect in Aberdeen* (Aberdeen, 1985).

S. Wood, J. Patrick, *History in the Grampian Landscape* (Aberdeen, 1982).

F. Wyness, *City by the Grey North Sea* (Aberdeen, 1966).

F. Wyness, *Aberdeen—Century of Change* (Aberdeen, 1975).

THE ECONOMY OF ABERDEEN

Robert E. Tyson

In that remarkable book, *The North-East Lowlands of Scotland* (1952), John Allan wrote:

> Aberdeen is a city in which nearly two hundred thousand people live and most of them earn a tolerable living. That is, perhaps, the most remarkable thing about the place. For Aberdeen is well beyond the northern limits of industrial Scotland, far from the coalfields and the iron foundries, and one of the largest cities to be found so far north ... When you look across from Kincorth at the shining walls of Aberdeen, and notice how infrequent the factory chimneys, you may think the town has no visible means of support. How then is Aberdeen the third city in Scotland—a position it held for so long, and now has won again? (p.109).

Given Aberdeen's location one might, indeed, have expected it to be one of those ancient towns—like Chester, Exeter, Shrewsbury or Worcester—which the industrial revolution passed by. It was the economic development of Aberdeen in the nineteenth century that prevented this from happening though the course of that development was far from smooth.

Although with far fewer people than when John Allan was writing, Aberdeen at the beginning of the nineteenth century was by contemporary standards a large town. Its population of 27,000 (which included not only the four quarters of St Nicholas parish but the adjacent suburbs) made it the sixteenth largest town in Great Britain (see Table 1). The rapid growth which had begun sometime in the second half of the eighteenth century continued until 1851, when with 72,000 inhabitants it was actually fourteenth. During the 1850s, however, there was hardly any growth at all. Not only was there a check to the

TABLE 1

The population of Aberdeen and ranking in size among British provincial towns, 1801-1911

	Population[1]	Increase over previous census (per cent)	Ranking[2]
1801	26,992	—	16
1811	34,640	28.3	13
1821	43,821	26.5	14
1831	56,681	29.5	11
1841	63,262	11.6	13
1851	71,973	13.8	14
1861	73,905	2.7	22
1871	88,198	19.5	22
1881	105,189	19.6	22
1891	124,943	17.5	24
1901	153,503	22.9	22
1911	163,891	6.8	21

Sources:
1. Hugh MacKenzie, *The Third Statistical Account of Scotland: The City of Aberdeen* (Edinburgh, 1953).
2. B. R. Mitchell and P. Deane, *Abstract of British Historical Statistics* (Cambridge, 1962), 24-7.

flow of immigrants from the countryside but almost certainly heavy emigration either to the rest of Great Britain or overseas, with the result that Aberdeen fell to twenty-second in the rankings in 1861. The last four decades of the nineteenth century saw the population grow rapidly once more, particularly in the 1880s and 90s and this was followed by another, though less serious, check between 1901 and 1911. At the latter date Aberdeen had 164,000 inhabitants or six times as many as in 1801 and had maintained its 1861 ranking. This performance is all the more impressive because, unlike Glasgow and Dundee, it owed hardly anything to Irish and Highland immigration. The great majority of those entering city came, as they had always done, from its hinterland, particularly rural Aberdeenshire.

The overall trend in population and of the city's economy, therefore, was one of substantial growth apart from the 1850s and the first decade of the twentieth century. The check of the 1850s is particularly important since it marks the boundary between two distinct periods of economic development. The first in fact started in 1779 when textiles began to be manufactured by the factory system which gradually replaced the traditional domestic industry of the countryside. By the end of the eighteenth century there were a number of factories within and around the city, the most important of which were Hadden and Company in the Green who manufactured stockings and other woollen goods, Leys, Masson and Company on the Don at Grandholm and Milne and Cruden in the Gallowgate, both of whom were manufacturers of linen, and Gordon, Barron and Company at Woodside, who produced cotton yarns and printed cloth. The industry continued to expand, and at its peak in 1840 employed 12,000 men, women and children in some of the largest industrial units in Britain. Aberdeen appeared well on the way to becoming a textile town.

With the onset of depression in the early 1840s, however, the industry began to experience considerable difficulties which became acute between 1848 and 1852. The result was a series of failures which saw only two firms (Richards and Company in linen and J. & J. Crombie in woollens) survive. Some three thousand workers lost their jobs in 1848 alone while in the industrial suburb of Woodside the failure of Leys, Masson and Company saw the income of the inhabitants reduced from £50,000 a year to £8,000. There was a partial recovery since some of the firms which went under were eventually replaced by new ones and when the British Association for the Advancement of Science met in Aberdeen in 1859 a survey of the city's economy revealed a basically prosperous textile industry though one which employed only about half as many workers as in 1840. Some of the firms, however, were still exceptionally large; Richards and Company, for example, employed 2,236 workers which made it a contemporary giant.

Nevertheless, the industry had received a blow from which it never really recovered. It managed to survive by specialising in particular lines such as Aberdeen 'winceys' but towards the end of the century underwent another period of contraction as a result of labour disputes and the McKinley tariff, which hit exports to the United States. Hadden's Mills and the Bannermill both closed in 1904 while Crombies and Richards survived only with considerable difficulty. Crombies were forced to abandon the American market and concentrate on selling their superb quality cloth to the Continent while Richards were rescued by a group of local businessmen. There was also an attempt to establish a jute industry though there was only ever one firm, albeit one which had over 2,000 employees. By contrast the Dundee jute industry, which had not existed until the 1830s, had 35,000 employees at that date.

Why the textile industry should have collapsed so dramatically in mid-century is not easy to explain. One immediate cause was the Hadden family's speculation in railway shares which led to the failure of their firm in 1848. The problem of the Aberdeen industry, however, went far beyond the financial embarrassment of some proprietors. The textile industry was becoming increasingly concentrated in a few favoured areas (Lancashire for cottons, the West Riding for woollens and worsteds, Northern Ireland for linen, Dundee for jute) where it could take full advantage of economies of scale not simply in the manufacture of textiles but also in the supply of raw materials, marketing of products and establishment of ancillary industries. Aberdeen's handicaps were beginning to be felt by about 1840, most obviously in the lack of cheap coal for steam-power, for which the limited water power site on the Don could not compensate. In 1840 it was estimated that the textile industry in and around Aberdeen generated 870 hp. by steam compared with only 660 hp. by water and that any further expansion would be dependent upon the former where Aberdeen was at a disadvantage. Aberdeen also suffered from high transport costs as a result of distance from raw materials and customers. It should be stressed, however, that what was happening to Aberdeen in the 1840s and early 1850s was part of a general trend which affected even the much better endowed Glasgow area; the distress in Paisley, for example, was far more acute than in Aberdeen.

The same problem occurred, though in a less dramatic form, in another long-established industry, that of shipbuilding. At the beginning of the nineteenth century Aberdeen was a major shipbuilding centre with no fewer than seven firms which in 1801 built forty two ships; this was more than any other Scottish port though the gross tonnage of 3,461 tons was exceeded by Glasgow and Leith. The introduction of steam-powered ships from the 1820s onwards, however, was a severe threat since Aberdeen, unlike the Clyde, did not have immediate access to coal and iron. One major firm, John Duffus and Company, actually ceased business in 1848, but otherwise Aberdeen's response was to remain with sail and specialise in building vessels for those long distance trades where steam was at a disadvantage. The result was the golden age of the clippers between 1850 and 1870 when superb ships with their 'Aberdeen Bow' like the *Thermopylae* and *Yangtse* won Aberdeen ship-builders an unrivalled reputation.

The advances in marine technology and the opening of the Suez Canal in 1869, however, ended this glorious if brief chapter since together they allowed steamships to capture the China and Australia trades. The advantage in shipbuilding now passed decisively to rivers which had immediate access to coal, iron and steel. Three long-established firms closed down or merged with others and the city's own shipping companies turned increasingly to the Clyde for their ships. However, Hall, Russell and Company began to build iron ships from 1867 onward and the industry managed to find a niche for itself. The building of sailing ships ceased altogether after 1885 and the industry concentrated on small cargo-passenger ships (the shallowness of the Dee limited their size to not more than 4,000 tons) and above all fishing trawlers, liners and drifters. It was the emergence of a large fishing industry towards the end of the nineteenth century which eventually provided the main source of demand and a replacement for the defunct clippers. In all, between 1886 and 1914 no fewer than 496 steam trawlers, 133 steam drifters and 23 steam liners were built, 54 per cent of the total tonnage launched on the Dee. Two-thirds of all trawlers were for North East owners but such was Aberdeen's reputation in this field that the remainder went not only to other ports of Scotland but to the major English fishing centres of Hull, Grimsby and Fleetwood, and even to France, Belgium, Ireland and Brazil. Employment in the industry more then held its own; in 1903 the three surviving firms employed 2,500 men (1,400 of them at Hall, Russell & Co.) compared with 2,000 in five firms in 1870. However, other shipbuilding rivers, notably the

Clyde and Tyne, had grown much more rapidly and thus Aberdeen declined into merely a minor centre of the industry. Between 1870 and 1914 its total output was only 337,790 tons compared with the Clyde's 16,279,936 during the same period.

The economic development of Aberdeen in the second half of the nineteenth century was not to be based on textiles or shipbuilding but on those industries which could take advantage of the natural resources of the North East. Development was not to be built around a single industry, as in the case of jute in Dundee, for a surprising variety of industries thrived in Aberdeen, some of them small and highly specialised.

One of the oldest of these was papermaking, whose origins in the North East went back to the seventeenth century. Strictly speaking, most of the industry's development took place beyond the city, for only one mill lay within its boundary. However, there were several large mills just outside, notably at Mugiemoss and Stoneywood, which relied on the city for labour, customers and transport. Initially these firms were attracted to the area by the availability of abundant supplies of fresh water (something, incidentally, that Dundee lacked) and because it was an untapped source of rags which were the main raw material. When esparto grass and wood-pulp began to be used from the 1860s onwards they could be imported through the port of Aberdeen. In Aberdeen, with its university, schools, printing firms, newspapers, law courts and offices, there was a large and growing local demand for the industry's products though the size of the firms, particularly Alexander Pirie's mill at Stoneywood, meant that everntually most of their output was exported. Although perhaps with greater local advantages the industry (which in 1886 employed 2,500 people) followed textiles in becoming increasingly specialised, with one firm, for example, concentrating on envelopes, and another on high-quality writing paper (which protected it from trade depressions).

Perhaps the most characteristic of all Aberdeen's industries, however, was granite in which it had no British rival. To a large extent the industry had begun as a by-product of agricultural improvement, using loose boulders cleared from reclaimed land to produce rough paving stones for local use and export to London (where they very often went as ballast in sailing ships).

By 1800 several quarries had opened up and were producing setts and paving stones of regular size and shape, together with blocks for constructional purposes. By 1821 exports of granite to London amounted to nearly 35,000 tons although most output probably went into the building of Aberdeen. The hardness of granite, which had delayed the opening of quarries and the use of the stone for building, also discouraged attempts to polish it but Alexander Macdonald's invention in the 1830s of machinery to dress and polish the stone brought a tremendous impetus to the industry with large numbers of granite polishing firms opening in the east end of the city. The building of a network of local railways after the middle of the century made it possible to move granite from inland Aberdeenshire, notably Kemnay, though in 1865 there were 20 quarries in operation in the Aberdeen area itself. Most of the Aberdeen labour force were engaged in polishing granite; at its peak in 1900 the industry employed 2,500 men and boys in ninety firms and there were a further 250 or so in quarries within the city boundary.

By this time the region was exporting something like 70,000 tons of granite a year, most of it through the port of Aberdeen, and the United States market was particularly important. Much of the output, however, was taken by Aberdeen for buildings and roads; the building cycle reached a peak in 1899 when 450 buildings were constructed in the city and this was followed by another one in 1904-5 (353 and 363 buildings respectively). Although still dominated by small firms, the industry had become more capital intensive and used an increasing amount of equipment to handle and shape the stone. Steam power for lifting, essential as quarries became deeper, began to be used from 1867 onwards. Like textiles, however, the industry experienced considerable difficulties just before the First World War. Tariffs and foreign competition hit exports while there was sharp downturn in building which led the local press in 1906 to comment on the numerous empty houses, low rents and virtual halt to new construction; the nadir was reached in 1912 when only thirteen houses were built.

The nineteenth century also saw a massive expansion in exports of agricultural products, most notably livestock and livestock products. As a result of the so-called 'agricultural revolution' which transformed the agriculture of the region between about 1780 and 1850, the port of Aberdeen began to send out considerable quantities first of oats and then cattle. Trade in the latter was the creation of the steamship in the 1820s. Before then cattle not intended for local consumption were sold lean and driven south, mainly to East Anglia where they were fattened for the London market or the Royal Navy. The introduction of regular steamship sailings to London made it profitable to export cattle which had been fattened. In 1847 nearly 16,000 live cattle left Aberdeen by sea and a further 1,800 as meat. It was the arrival of a continuous rail link between London and Aberdeen early in 1849, however, which led to the dramatic rise of the meat trade, since the rail journey took thirty-six hours compared with forty-eight by sea and was less subject to delays. The railway was more suited to carrying perishables, particularly dead meat, and by 1860 transported 5,769 tons of this commodity compared with only fifty-three tons by sea.

In 1870 it was calculated that 65,000 cattle a year were passing through the Aberdeen markets of which 26,000 beasts, mainly of inferior quality, were consumed locally, 11,000 exported live by rail or ship, and the remaining 28,000 slaughtered in Aberdeen and sent south by rail as 8,000 tons of beef. At that date Aberdeenshire beef fetched the highest price on the London market, partly because of the skill of the Aberdeen butchers of whom it was said that 'there are no others who know the beasts for the London market equal to the Aberdeen butchers and from no other place does it arrive in the same condition'.

In Aberdeen were the cattle markets and slaughter houses that made the meat trade possible, together with a host of subsidiary industries such as chemical fertiliser plants and agricultural implement makers. Other industries used by-products such as hide and tallow works, fat refineries and perhaps most spectacularly of all, the comb industry. In 1830 John Stewart moved from Edinburgh to Aberdeen to be nearer supplies of horn and by 1854 was producing nine million combs a year in a factory employing 700 men, boys and girls: by the beginning of this century output had risen to an incredible twenty-five million combs, though such was the demand for horn that by this time most was imported from abroad.

The high quality of Aberdeen's meat, together with a prejudice in favour of the home product and rising real incomes, meant that the beef industry withstood the onset of foreign imports from the 1870s onwards better than other agricultureal products. Even here the output of oats for the enormous and growing number of horses meant that North East's other main agricultural export fared better than wheat and flour. In the early 1880s Aberdeen had five flour mills which used wheat grown in the North East or imported in the Baltic but by the end of the century all had closed down. The region had more or less abandoned wheat farming and there was intense competition from huge mills in London, Liverpool and Glasgow which used American or Canadian wheat.

It was not shipbuilding, paper, granite or food processing which replaced textiles as Aberdeen's most important industry in the second half of the nineteenth century but fishing. It is surprising how long it took for Aberdeen to become a major fishing port. There had always been some fishing all the year out of the tiny settlements of Footdee and Torry but attempts to expand it had never been successful and as late as 1880 few of the boats that took part in the summer fishing belonged to Aberdeen or the nearby fishing communities. There was also the occasional trawler from England landing fish from nearby waters. The industry at that date employed fewer than 400 men and women and the value of white fish landings was about £10,000. This was for local consumption, and salmon was still the main fish export.

In 1882, however, a few local businessmen purchased the steam-tug *Toiler* 'for the purpose of prosecuting trawling' and at the end of six months fishing were able to declare a dividend of 100%. Within a decade Aberdeen became the largest white-fish port in Scotland, accounting for something like 20% of the total catch. It had thirty-eight trawlers of its own, there were landings by trawlers from other ports, and line boats from elsewhere made the port their base. The reasons for this success are not hard to find. Successive improvements to the port, particularly the completion of the Albert Basin in 1870, the existence of shipyards and repair facilities, a large local market and rail lines to the rest of Britain, and good fishing grounds in Aberdeen Bay and adjacent parts of the North Sea combined to make the city an obvious major fishing centre.

Although the North Sea was always the most important area, during the 1890s Aberdeen trawlers began to venture into grounds where there was less advantage of proximity such as the Northern Isles, Faroes and Iceland, the Minch and Atlantic. Nevertheless, fish landed from them in Aberdeen was able to reach London more quickly than fish from the same grounds landed in the rival ports of Hull or Grimsby. In 1890 most of the fish arriving in Aberdeen was cured and sales to London were small though the railway companies had started to run daily fish trains from the mid 1880s onwards. However, the growing volume of landings meant an increase in fish of types which could not be cured, particularly flat fish, and London was the obvious market. The cost of such a long rail journey made a substantial addition to the price but this was more than outweighted by the high price which it commanded in London because of its quality. Fish landed at Hull and Grimsby spent longer at sea and therefore suffered a greater deterioration. However, haddock for curing was still the most important fish sold in the Aberdeen market.

The expansion into more northerly waters inevitably meant greater competition from other ports and increased operating costs. Trawlers needed to be larger and more powerful, fuel bills were higher, more time was lost travelling to and from distant grounds. However despite these problems growth continued unrestricted, as Table 2 shows; in 1900 Aberdeen had 100 trawlers, and on the eve of the First World War, when the port accounted for 70% of Scottish white-fish landings, no fewer than 218. By the latter date it was the largest of Aberdeen's industries although most of those employed in it worked on shore processing fish, repairing and building boats and supplying the fishing fleet with all its requirements, from groceries and coal to boxes and ice. The *Aberdeen Free Press* estimated in 1905 that 9,200 persons were employed in this way, of whom 3,000 were in the highly seasonal herring industry and the remainder were full time. Although the fishermen themselves were a minority, their numbers also rose dramatically to reach just over 3,000. This suggests that at that date something like 12,000 people (nearly 18% of the labour force) were engaged in the fishing industry. However, this number does not include many others who in one way or another earned at least part of

TABLE 2
Fish landings (cwts) in Aberdeen, 1888-1912

Year ending 30 September	Fish landed (cwt)
1888	133,180
1892	332,240
1896	532,200
1900	911,260
1904	1,463,640
1908	1,994,620
1912	2,256,960

Source:
Hugh MacKenzie, The Third Statistical Account of Scotland: The City of Aberdeen (Edinburgh, 1953), 164.

their livelihood from the industry—those employed, for example in insurance companies, shops, building and the professions. Like the oil industry today, the fishing industry at its peak touched almost every section of the economy. Hugh MacKenzie estimated that in 1920, when the industry directly employed 12,000 (about the same as in 1914), something like 40,000 men, women and children or 25% of the population earned their livelihood from the fish trade and this may not be an exaggeration.

Nevertheless, one distinguishing feature of the Aberdeen economy was its diversity. Even fish never quite had the importance of textiles in 1840 when the latter industry, as we have seen, also employed about 12,000 workers although the total labour force was very much smaller. Another distinguishing feature was the importance of local resources—the produce of land and sea—to the economic development of the city. Even an industry like engineering, which in 1911 employed 2,941 was to a considerable extent dependent upon paper, granite and fishing for its customers (though Aberdeen investment in the Far East also led to the manufacture of tea, rice and coffee machinery). The emphasis in most of these industries was on quality, whether it be Crombie cloth, Aberdeen-Angus beef, granite memorials or superb writing paper. The growth of incomes in the nineteenth century, not only in Britain but abroad as well, and more sophisticated tastes created an expanding market for these products while the improvement in Aberdeen's transport facilities meant that the city was able to meet this demand. However, steamships and railways could sometimes be a double edged weapon since they also exposed the north-east to competition from outside, as can be seen in the case of flour milling.

The reliance on local resources—water, stone, beef, fish— produced an industrial development different from that of the other Scottish cities. The extractive industries of granite and fishing (as Table 3 shows) were far more important than else- where while manufacturing industries were correspondingly less important than in Dundee and Glasgow and almost the same as in Edinburgh. Economic growth in the nineteenth century is usually discussed in terms of the great Victorian staple indus- tries of textiles, coal, iron and steel, shipbuilding and heavy engineering, but in Aberdeen these industries either did not exist or were comparatively small. In 1911, for example, textiles employed only 6.9% of the labour force (compared with a staggering 48.2% in Dundee) and shipbuilding and the metal industries combined only 7.6% (see Table 4). However, many

TABLE 3

Distribution of employment in major Scottish cities in 1911

	Dundee	Edinburgh	Glasgow	Aberdeen
Extractive industries	1.4	2.7	1.7	13.9
Manufacturing industries	66.7	32.4	48.0	36.4
Service industries	29.7	60.0	46.3	45.5
unclassified	2.6	4.9	4.1	4.3
Total	100.4	100.0	100.1	100.1

Source:
A. M. Carstairs 'The nature and diversification of employment in Dundee in the twentieth century', in S. J. Jones (ed.) *Dundee and district* (Dundee, 1968), 320.

TABLE 4

Employment in Aberdeen industries, 1911

Rank	Industry	No. employed
1	Fishing	6,009
2	Textiles	4,725
3	Clothing	3,948
4	Metals	3,472
5	Building	3,226
6	Granite	2,378
7	Wood and furniture	1,995
8	Paper	1,831
9	Shipbuilding	1,724
10	Food & Drink	1,419

Source:
Census of Scotland, 1911.

of those in the manufacturing sector such as tailors, shoemakers and cabinet makers still worked at home or in small workshops very much as their predecessors had done in earlier centuries, while the methods of building industry, which employed over 3,000 workers, were still largely unchanged.

What Table 3 demonstrates above all, however, is the importance of the service sector (transport, trade and commerce, the professions and domestic service) which employed nearly half the labour force; domestic servants alone accounted for nearly 10% of the total, more than any single industry except fishing. Much of the growth of this sector was obviously a direct consequence of the rise of industry but it also stemmed from Aberdeen's traditional role as the regional capital of the North East of Scotland. The university, banks, insurance companies, law firms, accountants, wholesalers and retailers, served not merely the city but its large hinterland and the same was true of the port and railway. The degree of enterprise here was every bit as great as in manufacturing. By the end of the nineteenth century, for example, Aberdeen was the only centre outside Edinburgh and Glasgow still to have its own bank (the North of Scotland and the Town and County, which eventually joined together in 1908) and the city was an important exporter of capital.

The contrast with Dundee, where fewer than 30% of the labour force were employed in services, is particularly striking. In 1911 the two cities had almost identical populations but Aberdeen had nearly three times as many lawyers, more than twice as many engineers, surveyors and bank officials, and considerably more physicians, dentists, teachers and insurance officials. It also had nearly twice as many domestic servants and people with private means. The earnings of professional people in this period when compared with manual workers were extremely high. Just before the First World War the highest paid worker in manufacturing earned less than £2 a week and many received under half this amount whereas the national average for the 'higher' professions such as medicine and law was £328 a year and for the 'lower' professions £155: even on the latter income it was possible to employ a servant.

The structure of the Aberdeen economy meant that it avoided the extremes of wealth that existed elsewhere. In Aberdeen there were no equivalents of the great Dundee textile dynasties such as the Coxes and the Baxters, but a large middle-class which included not only the professions but many ship-owners, fish curers, granite merchants etc. It was the existence of this extensive middle-class which explains why Aberdeen was a relatively wealthy city which compared more than favourably with most English equivalents when measured by one of the best indicators of wealth, *per capita* Schedule D income tax. In 1880 London was the wealthiest city in Britain, with £25.4 tax paid per head of population, followed by Manchester (£24.9), Edinburgh (£21.1), Liverpool (£20.0) and Glasgow (£16.7). The equivalent for Aberdeen was £9.3 which made it the tenth wealthiest provincial town, not far behind Birmingham, Bristol and Nottingham and well ahead of Leeds, Leicester and Sheffield (see Table 5). Dundee, with £8.4, was twelfth which was surprisingly high in view of its small middle class. Perhaps the best indication of Aberdeen's middle-class wealth, however, was its magnificent west end and the villas that stretched along the North Deeside Road.

What of the working classes, who paid no Schedule D income tax? On the whole wage-rates in Aberdeen were somewhat lower than in Edinburgh, Glasgow and even Dundee though in the case of the last this was more than compensated by

TABLE 5

Schedule D Assessments of London and largest British provincial towns, 1879-80

Rank	Town	Per capita assessment (£)
1	London	25.4
2	Manchester	24.9
3	Edinburgh	21.1
4	Liverpool	20.0
5	Glasgow	16.7
6	Newcastle	12.8
7	Bristol	11.2
8	Bradford	10.7
9	Nottingham	10.3
10	Birmingham	10.0
<u>11</u>	<u>Aberdeen</u>	<u>9.3</u>
12	Brighton	9.0
13	Dundee	8.4
14	Leeds	8.0
15	Hull	7.5
	Leicester	7.5
17	Sheffield	7.1
	Stoke	7.1
19	Sunderland	7.0
20	Bolton	6.8
21	Swansea	5.9
22	Oldham	5.2
23	Salford	4.9
24	Wednesbury	4.3
25	Portsmouth	4.2
26	Blackburn	3.8
27	Wolverhampton	2.7

Source:

W. D. Rubinstein, 'The Victorian Middle Classes: Wealth, Occupation and Geography', *Economic History Review* xxx, 4 (1977), 617.

Aberdeen having somewhat lower rents and prices. What is important, however, is not so much how earnings for a particular occupation compared with those elsewhere but how many people were occupied in that group. One of the problems that faced the Aberdeen working class was that many jobs were in occupations that did not pay particularly high wages. The best paid workers in Britain tended to be in coalmining, iron and steel, heavy engineering and shipbuilding (which resulted in Clydeside becoming a high wage area on the eve of the First World War), not granite, paper or fishing. Aberdeen fish workers, for example, earned only $3\frac{1}{2}d$. an hour or about 16 shillings a week. This problem, though, was nothing like as acute as in Dundee where nearly half the labour force was employed in the jute industry. Textiles generally were a lowly paid occupation and wages in jute were the lowest of any branch, being only about two-thirds of those in the Lancashire cotton industry. Moreover, the great majority of those employed in jute were women and children, which explains why females in Dundee made up a much greater proportion of the labour force than in Aberdeen (where the percentage of married women employed was the lowest of any Scottish city). In Dundee eight times as many married women worked as in Aberdeen and some of them were the principal breadwinners since men there often found it difficult to obtain work.

It is the generally lower level of earnings in Dundee which largely explains why almost every social statistic available compares unfavourably with Aberdeen, whether infant mortality, school attendance or housing density. Housing conditions in Aberdeen, particularly in the Gallowgate area, could be as bad as anywhere in Scotland but overall were considerably better than in Dundee and Glasgow. For example in 1911 38.7% of Aberdonians lived in one or two room dwellings, slightly more than in Edinburgh, but in Glasgow the comparable figure was 62.4% and in Dundee 63.1%.

In developing a more diversified economy from the 1850s onwards, particularly one not so dependent upon textiles, Aberdeen had followed a more beneficial path than Dundee, though this may not have seemed obvious to contemporaries until the 1880s. Despite the importance of fish, Aberdeen did not place its economic eggs in one basket and therefore avoided the dangers that over-commitment brought with it, notably severe trade depressions. From 1880 onwards Aberdeen grew more rapidly than any other Scottish city, even Glasgow, and the immigrants who poured in still came from its hinterland, including for the first time the fishing communities between Peterhead to the north and Inverbervie to the south. This movement came

TABLE 6

Index of daily rate of building wages (carpenters), 1795-1906 (London = 100)

	c.1795	c.1843	1886	1906
London	100	100	100	100
Exeter	62	—	61	71
Manchester	88	87	89	91
Glasgow	48	60	83	91
Edinburgh	48	65	72	86
Aberdeen	43	48	67	76

Source:
E. H. Hunt, 'Industrial and Regional Inequality: Wages in Britain, 1760-1914', *Journal of Economic History*, xliv, 4 (1986).

to a halt in the first decade of this century when some sectors of the economy faltered and there was quite heavy emigration.

Between 1851 and 1911 the labour force of Aberdeen grew by over 36,000, a clear demonstration that economic growth in the Victorian age was not dependent upon iron and coal. There is also evidence that it was accompanied by a rise in the standard of living more rapid than in many other areas of Britain. At the opening of century building wages (usually regarded as a reasonable indication of wages generally) in Aberdeen were only 43% of those in London; by 1886 they had risen to 67% as large and by 1906 to 76% (see Table 6) and were higher than in much of England and Wales. The way in which the gap was closed is evidence of considerable economic growth.

When compared with earlier centuries, the economic development of Aberdeen between 1800 and 1914 was indeed remarkable, particularly when its handicaps are taken into account, though it must be emphasised that conditions were much more favourable than in, say, the inter-war years when the economy stagnated. Only with the arrival of oil did Aberdeen regain the kind of growth that had characterised the 'great century'.

BIBLIOGRAPHY

J.N. Bartlett, 'Alexander Pirie & Sons of Aberdeen and the expansion of the British paper industry, c.1860-1914', *Business History*, xxii (1980).

G.B. Bothwell, 'On the Manufactures and Trade of Aberdeen', *Report of the Twenty-ninth Meeting of the British Association for the Advancement of Science* (London, 1860).

I.F. Carter, *Farm Life in North-East Scotland, 1840-1914* (Edinburgh, 1979).

G. Channon, 'The Aberdeenshire beef trade with London: a study in steamship and railway competiton, 1850-69', *Transport History*, ii (1969).

J. Cruickshank, *Alexander Pirie and Sons Ltd* (Aberdeen, 1946).

W. Diack, *Rise and Progress of the Granite Industry in Aberdeen* (Aberdeen, 1950).

T. Donnelly, The Development of the Aberdeen Granite Industry 1750-1939 (Unpublished PhD. thesis, University of Aberdeen, 1976).

T. Donnelly, 'Shipbuilding in Aberdeen, 1750-1914', *Northern Scotland* iv (1981).

A.J. Durie, 'Balanced and Unbalanced Urban Economies: Aberdeen and Dundee, 1800-1914' *Scotia-American-Canadian Journal of Scottish Studies*, viii (1984).

M. Gray, *The Fishing Industries of Scotland 1790-1914* (Aberdeen, 1978).

S.J. Jones (ed.), *Dundee and District* (Dundee, 1963).

C.H. Lee, 'Some Aspects of the Coastal Shipping Trade: The Aberdeen Steam Navigation Company, 1835-1880', *Journal of Transport History*, iii (1975-6).

H. MacKenzie, *Third Statistical Account of Aberdeen* (Edinburgh, 1953).

R.C. Michie, 'Trade and Transport in the Economic Development of North-East Scotland in the Nineteenth Century', *Scottish Economic and Social History*, iii (1983).

J.H. Smith, 'The Cattle Trade of Aberdeenshire in the Nineteenth Century', *Agricultural History Review*, iii (1955).

W. Watt, 'Fifty Years' Progress in Aberdeen', *Transactions of the Aberdeen Philosphical Society*, iv (1910).

NO MEAN ABERDONIANS—SOME ABERDEEN ENTREPRENEURS

Bernard Maitland Balfour

Aberdeen, like Rome can claim to be built on seven hills, but unlike Rome can make no claim to have had a visit from St Paul, one of the early Apostles, or any other saint to my knowledge although we did have until recently a St Paul Street now demolished, to make way for the new Bon Accord Centre. However, Aberdonians can, like St Paul claim to be 'a citizen of no mean City'.

'The Granite City' has long been one of the many titles applied to Aberdeen, but it is really only in the last two hundred years that such a description has been true. Before that time, most of the larger buildings, including West St Nicholas (rebuilt as late as 1750) and of course King's College were built of sandstone, either from Covesea on the Moray Coast or Kildrummy. If not of sandstone, the poorer buildings would be of wattle and daub, as has been shown in the excavations in the Broad Street and Drum's Lane areas.

However, granite was certainly being used outside 'The Granite City' in such ancient buildings as Crathes and Drum Castles on Deeside, and Midmar and Castle Fraser on Donside, some of which date back to Norman times. And, nearer home, St Machar's Cathedral, was built in its present granite form over six hundred years ago.

Visitors to the Pyramids in Egypt are, quite rightly, amazed at what Ancient Egyptian workmen were able to achieve with the most rudimentary tools and lifting gear, and here in Aberdeen we too should marvel at what our ancestors built with the simplest of resources. Without the quarries available to the

Ancient Egyptians, the Aberdonians of medieval times simply gathered together rough granite boulders from the sea-shore, or from the fields, the latter moved to allow the 'twal-oosen ploo' room to turn over the soil. From these sources came the early granite castles and cathedral which still stand today. However, granite really only came into common use for building when the first quarries were opened for this purpose. Among the earliest of such quarries used for the building of the city of Aberdeen was the Dancing Cairns quarry, at Scatterburn, which later supplied the portico for the Music Hall, and in 1840 the statue of the Duke of Gordon, which in my youth stood in the Castlegate, and in my old age now stands in Golden Square. This statue, it was claimed, was the first granite statue to be erected since the time of the Ptolemys in Egypt.

Another quarry was opened up in the middle of the eighteenth century by James Elmslie in Rosemount. It was the Loanhead quarry and the name is still there in Loanhead Terrace and Loanhead Place. If anyone wants to see samples of Loanhead granite, have a look at Robert Gordon's College, or the Denburn Church in Summer Street, or the old Royal Infirmary in Woolmanhill. All date from around the middle of the eighteenth century.

If asked to name any one quarry, most Aberdonians would answer, 'Rubislaw'. It has been described as 'the hole Aberdeen came out of' — and that is a good description. But not only did it supply Aberdeen's needs, it also supplied the needs of many other users throughout Britain, and in fact throughout the world.

When the Industrial Revolution needed improved harbours to handle the products of the new machine age, and the Public Health Acts demanded better houses and the paving of streets, there was a great demand for granite. Rubislaw granite was especially requested to pave the streets of London. For centuries the London streets had wooden blocks or cobbles on them. It was Rubislaw 'cassies' or 'setts' which replaced them over the years. All done by hand, of course, by men called 'paviors' who 'dunted' in the stones by sheer brute force.

Rubislaw, of course, was part of the land given to the city by King Robert the Bruce — and the rent was — one silver penny — and only when asked for! The city 'fathers' in their wisdom leased it out when they were advised that the granite was not of good enough quality.

It was when Rubislaw was leased to John Gibb, one of the early Aberdeen granite entrepreneurs, that it really began to pay dividends. At one time horses would pull the 'cube stone' up a winding road to the top of the quarry. A big step forward came when steam power was applied to quarrying. Another leading figure in the granite industry, John Fyfe of Kemnay, used a steamdriven, derrick-crane for lifting, and a steam-hammer for splitting stone. Fyfe also introduced a cable-way which was used to hoist a skip with the cut stone.

The wire which was stretched across the quarry was soon nicknamed. Charles Blondin was a famous tight-rope walker, who had crossed the Niagara Falls trundling a wheel-barrow in front of him. He then did it in the reverse direction—on stilts! Blondin came to Aberdeen in 1861 and performed his tight-rope feats on a wire over Golden Square. Thus when a similar wire was put across any quarry it was therefore named a 'Blondin'.

Nobody to public knowledge has tried to walk over the 'Blondin' at Rubislaw quarry, but there is a story that a pre-1939 university student went across hand over hand, and tied his handkerchief in the middle to prove it. The same student is, allegedly, the one who climbed the spire of the Mitchell Tower and tied a skeleton to the top, complete with top hat.

Of course, nowadays, the streets of London are no longer covered in Aberdeen granite. But some of the pavements still are. Just over one hundred years ago, in 1885, the Adamant Stone and Paving Company was set up at Bucksburn for the production of artificial stone for paving purposes. The basic material is finely-crushed granite and Ferrocrete cement, and at one time the careful observer could see the name 'Adamant' on the paving slabs in brass letters.

Not only did Aberdeen supply 'cassies' and paving-slabs, for another Aberdeen entrepreneur, Alexander McDonald, in 1820 began polishing granite. According to tradition, he had seen examples of Ancient Egyptian polished granite in the British Museum and after many experiments he produced a satisfactory finish on Aberdeen granite. In 1832 the first polished granite monument from McDonald's Works in Constitution Street was sent to Kensal Green Cemetery in London. Other entrepreneurs soon followed his lead and the monumental and architectural side of the granite business had started.

Most people if asked can only distinguish two shades of granite—mainly grey and mainly pinkish. But depending on where the granite comes from there is quite a variety of colours. For instance, near Peterhead there was the Cairngall quarry—it produced a dark blue granite and was used for the tombs of Queen Victoria and Prince Albert at Frogmore, Windsor. Cairngall is also on the tomb of Napoleon III, as well as on the Paris Opera House. Persley quarry granite is light grey and can be seen on the Nurses' Home at Woodend, as well as on the Bank at the east corner of Union Street and St Nicholas Street. Dancing Cairns quarry granite was used in the building of the Thames Embankment, Old London Bridge, and Trafalgar Square.

Probably one of the most easily recognisable granites is from Peterhead. It is a warm reddish-brown colour and was much used in London. It can be seen on the Stock Exchange, and on the Foreign Office. In fact Peterhead granite even went as far as Imperial Russia, where it was used for a statue of Catherine the Great.

The spire of the Mitchell Tower, which the nameless student climbed in the dark, was made of Kemnay granite, that silver-grey granite with a touch of brown which can also be seen in the Salvation Army Citadel, HM Theatre, and of course in the Aberden Town House which was originally to be built in brick as it was thought impossible to get enough granite. Fyfe at Kemnay proved otherwise.

Aberdeen's Town House leads to the name of the next Aberdeen entrepreneur—Alexander Anderson, who died a hundred years ago, in 1887. As the *Aberdeen Journal* said of him at the time 'He was the man to whom Aberdeen is indebted'. Although born in Strichen in 1802, a son of the manse, he came to Aberdeen as a pupil of the old Schoolhill Grammar School, and then went on to Marischal College. He later entered the law profession and local politics—hence the Town House connection—and if Aberdonians are indebted to any one man for the foundation of the 'Granite City' as we know it today, it is to Alexander Anderson.

An uncle having left legacies for a House of Refuge for poor people and a Reformatory for difficult youngsters, Anderson caused Oldmill (now part of Woodend Hospital) and Oakbank (now a list D school) to be built. This launch into Aberdeen's affairs was quickly followed by the setting up of the North of Scotland Insurance Company in 1837 (where most of us met our dates at one time—'the Monkey Hoose') at the corner of Union Terrace, later the Northern Assurance Company, as well as the North of Scotland Bank, at the corner of Castle Street and King Street. The year 1838 saw the promotion of the Aberdeen Market Company and the later building of the New Market. The Market buildings were opened to the public on 30 April 1842, and by an unfortunate coincidence were burned to the ground exactly forty years later on 30 April 1882. Shortly after the Market was established Anderson started a Gas Company which was eventually taken over by the Corporation. Anderson was also closely connected with the Great North of Scotland Railway Company—'The little but good', as well as with the Deeside Railway and the Buchan line of the GNSR, both now defunct. Perhaps it is better to pass swiftly over Anderson's business connections with his cousin George Smith, better known to posterity as Chicago Smith, the founder of the Illinois Investment Company in the USA, whom unwise Aberdonians financed to the tune of some £100,000. The money finished up in Smith's growing fortune, and he died at the age of ninety-one leaving £5 million—but not to the citizins of Aberdeen. He did however leave money for the Smith Prize to the school children of Old Deer, his birth place, as a reminder of his success, however achieved.

In 1859 Anderson was diverted from his business activities into local politics. He was soon called to high office as Lord Provost, and in seven years had caused the waterworks at Cairnton to be opened, the whole sewage systems to be overhauled, new roads to be laid, and the building of a new Grammar School in 1865. As mentioned earlier, it is to him that the present Town House owes its existence. In 1863 he became Sir Alexander Anderson and is probably best remembered today in the street which so resembles him—fast, wide, and dangerous to cross—Anderson Drive.

When Anderson was associated with the North of Scotland

Bank, one of his co-directors was another Aberdeen entrepreneur—George Thompson, although like Sir Alexander, he was not a native born Aberdonian. However, his mother did come from Rubislaw, and he arrived in Aberdeen in 1806 at the age of two and lived here all the rest of his life, some ninety years until 1895.

Before the coming of Anderson's railways, the bulk of long distance trade from Aberdeen and the North East was carried by sea in locally built smacks. Aberdeen has always been one of the leading shipbuilding centres in Scotland but when George Thompson set up in business in Marischal Street in 1825 as a shipowner, among other things, one of the most splendid eras in Aberdeen's maritime history was about to begin. Of course there had been some sort of shipbuilding in Aberdeen since the very earliest times, even though it was of the most basic type. One of the first shipbuilders mentioned was Alexander Davidson who, in 1606 was given permission to clear-up the old cemetery of the Trinitarians (The Red Friars) and use it as a shipbuilding yard. It was usually from timber floated down the Dee that the early boats or 'snaws' constructed. A connection with the 'snaws' was said to be with the 'Snawie' Kirk (the parish church of Old Aberdeen), it being maintained from a levy on the cargoes of these small ships. However, this nice old tradition appears to have no foundation in history—St Mary ad Nives (St Mary of the Snows) was not founded by the good Bishop Elphinstone until the end of the fifteenth century.

Thompson's White Star Line, or Aberdeen Line for short, engaged A Hall and Company to build such ships for them as the *Scottish Maid* and *Cairngorm*, to beat the Yankees at the tea-carrying trade. But it was from the yard of Walter Hood and Company, in which Thompson was the principal partner, that perfection was produced. In the middle decade of the nineteenth century, Hood's built *Jerusalem*, *Pericles*, *Salamis*, and in 1868 *Thermopylae*, which was their crowning glory. She was probably the fastest sailing ship of all time, with a record day's run of 380 statute miles. Only the Clyde-built *Cutty Sark* was her equal and she was designed by Hercules Linton, who was born in Inverbervie and was trained in Aberdeen!

George Thompson, like Alexander Anderson, entered local politics and, like Anderson, became Lord Provost. During his spell in office he saw to alterations and improvements at the harbour and had the honour to welcome Queen Victoria and Prince Albert in September 1848, on their first visit to Balmoral. He was 'no mean Aberdonian' in the best sense, in that he left money to many Aberdeen institutions including the Royal Infirmary and the university.

The Aberdeen entrepreneurs mentioned so far all made their fortune at home, but one had to travel 'gey far afield' to make his—to Japan. If any Aberdonian happens to be just about three miles outside Nagasaki, on the coast road, they will find there a large bungalow, just over a hundred years old. At one time it was thatched but now its roof is covered in blue grey tiles. Unlike the rest of the houses it doesn't look onto the bay but faces the Mitsubishi shipyards. There is a memorial plate on the house which says that the original owner of the house, 'contributed in no small way to the development of Japan'.

The owner and first resident of the house was an 'Aiberdeen Loon' from the Bridge of Don. His name was Thomas Blake Glover, born in 1838, and his father was Lieutenant Tom Glover, superintendent of the coast guard station at Bridge of Don. Young Tom, then aged about twenty-two, went to Japan with his brother Alfred as representatives of a well-known Aberdeen firm, Crombies of Grandholm, still in existence, who made very excellent but expensive woollen material. Eventually the brothers prospered and set up on their own. They began the trawling industry in Japan. They set up the dockyards, and bought a locomotive from Shanghai, thus introducing railways to Japan. In this they were assisted by another Aberdonian—Annand by name, whose family, like Glover's, still live in the city.

Tom did not forget his hometown of Aberdeen either. When the Japanese government wanted to develop its own navy, Tom Glover persuaded them in 1868 to order a ship from Alexander Hall in Aberdeen. She was the *Ho Sho Maru* (or *Whirlwind*), and she was unique for those days by having a propeller as well as sails.

While she was being built, fire broke out in a timber-store near to Hall's shipbuilding yards and James Hall, one of the partners fearing that the fire might reached the Japanese warship found the news so alarming, that he dropped dead. The

Whirlwind left Aberdeen on 25 July 1869. She was of the most modern design, with muzzle-loading cannons at the bow and stern.

The new Japanese warship may have been called *Whirlwind* but her progress home hardly resembled her name. At her launch her propellor struck a stern post and she had to have a new one fitted. Then she lost her anchor and a fire broke out in her coal bunkers. However, she overcame all of these misfortunes so easily that the Japanese government were very impressed with their new warship. Later Hall's built other ships for the Japanese Navy. But of course the Japanese steadily acquired shipbuilding expertise, until they have, nowadays, the largest shipbuilding yards in the world.

However, Thomas Blake Glover, from the Bridge of Don, doesn't exactly disappear into the mists of history, never to be heard again. In fact Glover became world famous, although not under his own name. Some years after Tom's death in Japan in 1911, the famous Italian composer Puccini, wrote an opera based on Glover's life. It was called *Madame Butterfly*. For Glover had married a local girl, and Puccini used this love affair between the West, with all its then modern technology, and the East, still stuck in its ancient customs, to show that in a clash of cultures someone is bound to be hurt.

However, as far as we're aware Glover was a most faithful husband to his Japanese wife, unlike the 'Lieutenant Pinkerton' of the opera. Puccini simply used Glover's link between East and West as a romantic basis for a wonderful opera. But curiously enough, the link between Glover's family and Aberdeen wasn't broken on his death. His son, who inherited the trawling business, bought an Aberdeen trawler, or *Smokey Joe* (so-called on account of the clouds of black smoke that came out of the funnel) just before the First World War in 1914, when of course, Japan was one of Britains' allies.

So if any North East reader happens to be in Nagasaki, Japan, just keep saying—'Aye Aye—Fit like, min' and you might just get an unexpected response from one of Tom Glover's Japanese descendents, 'Ah-so, Ye ken!'—Aberdonian enterprise gets everywhere!

ABERDEEN'S ARCHITECTURE—FROM CLASSIC TO CALEDONIAN

William Brogden

Despite its antiquity and its recently much touted role as oil capital of Europe, Aberdeen is essentially a city of the nineteenth century. Like the century, it presents a number of contrasting, even mutually exclusive, ideas and conditions including opulence in the presence of unspeakable squalor, cruel selfishness and amazing charity. In architectural and urban design, the nineteenth century, and Aberdeen, presents the problem of appropriate style: classic purity or gothic complexity? Is an appeal to the universal better, or should we prefer something more particular, something more local? These concerns are far from unique to Aberdeen: however, the effects of the struggles with these concerns are unique. They gave the city its character, and a new style.

When I first came to Aberdeen I knew little about it except that it was built of granite and that the monarch chose to live in the area when she did not have to. I thought that particularly strange. Why should her ancestor the great Victoria, have chosen to live in Aberdeenshire, and in a modern 'castle'?

The Scotch Baronial or Scottish Baronial, or, as it was sometimes called in the nineteenth century, the Old Scotch Style, has only recently been accorded anything like legitimacy. Even now, my colleagues further south, and on the east coast of America and in Europe, do not really accord to the Scottish Baronial style the respect they should.[1] This paper traces its development, identifies some causes for it, and shows how it makes Aberdeen essentially what Aberdeen is,—that nice mixture of the stern (of the rational if you like) and the romantic.

If you stand outside Archibald Simpson's[2] Assembly Rooms

45

on Union Street, with its classical Greek porch of marvellous granite shafts with Ionic[3] capitals, and look up the street towards the old city, Aberdeen proper, what do you see but Tinkerbell's castle masquerading as the Salvation Army citadel! It is by any stretch of the imagination an extraordinary building, and in the light of the ways in which Aberdeen started developing architecturally in the late eighteenth century, it may seem that it should not exist. So I will try to explain why it does exist.

The eighteenth century, by application of reason and hard thinking, sought to establish rules, natural rules, beyond dispute, about things and activities. This clear-sighted and hard-headed approach is particularly associated, and reasonably so, with Scotland. Architecture had the light of reasoned enquiry shone upon it, but it must be admitted that the eighteenth century did not accord it a specially prominent place in the list of important things. In fact its role as an art was somewhat debatable: generally it was accepted that architecture was a useful art, and its utilitarian qualities were stressed: those essentially eighteenth century notions of the simple, plain and unaffected describe the light, airy and often severely box-like Georgian house. As Lord Kames,[4] the great Scottish aesthetician and lawyer, put it somewhat conventionally 'regularity and proportion are essential in building destined chiefly or solely to please the eye, because they are the means to produce an intrinsic beauty'. All buildings should exhibit these qualities. The expression of magnificence in fine architectural detail or the classical orders should be reserved for civic buildings or perhaps the residence of a great man, whom the eighteenth century was apt to grant an almost civic status.

Perhaps, too, churches could be admitted to this category, although Kames, like his age, was somewhat doubtful: a church, after all, was simply a convenient place where folk gathered to worship God, and its form should answer that criterion rather than attempt to embody or suggest any God-like qualities. So maybe it was to dignify Aberdeen and its council that the new West Kirk of St Nicholas was allowed to be not only proportionable and regular but to a degree magnificent as well (plate 7). It was designed by our native son James Gibbs,[5] in the early 1740s and carried on in the 1750s by Wyllie.[6]

The more utilitarian view of architecture is seen in Aberdeen from about the 1760s onwards in the works of people like William Law[7], who is thought to be the architect of 17 Castle Street. It was one of the new model tenements[8] with identical sash windows regularly disposed: the building is constructed of granite with part of a classical order used as detail at the eaves.

As rational enquiry could improve ordinary houses so it could be used to improve the town itself. As the Shiprow was too steep and crooked to give convenient access from the Castlegate to the recently improved harbour, it was decided to make a new street to solve the problem. In Marischal Street, built from 1767, we see the first application of entrepreneurial and engineering skills to solve a perceived urban problem. The easy gradient of the roadway, carried over Virginia Street by a bridge built by William Law, connected the heart of the town to the quayside. It not only made trade and commerce easier to carry on but, as it was lined with handsome granite houses, it was an ornament to Aberdeen as well. These houses, similar to 17 Castle Street, are of three stories, their entrances in the centre between purpose-built shops, with ten identical sash windows symmetrically arranged above. The architects, and it is stretching a point to call them such, were probably Law (in one case at least), William Dauney[9] and William Smith,[10] best known as father of the more famous John Smith.[11]

It was in a similar utilitarian frame of mind that a town meeting of 1794 sought from Charles Abercrombie,[12] an engineer then engaged in the turnpike roads to north and south, a report on the best means to connect crowded, congested Aberdeen with its crooked streets to its hinterland. He advised opening up two new streets, the first was to run from the Castlegate just east of the New Inn northwards towards the Don, while the second (and grander) street was to emerge from the Castlegate and run to the west, taking in Hunter's Row, cutting through St Katherine's Hill, and thence on a vaulted causeway (like Marischal Street) to the Denburn, which Abercrombie proposed crossing with a bridge to join the open ground west of the town.

The New Streets Trustees advertised for designs from architects all over Britain in 1799. Of these only James Young's unsuccessful entry survives (plate 8). It, and presumably the others, illustrates a desire to enlarge the scope of architecture from one house to a genuinely civic scale as had already occurred in Britain in Bath, and more recently in Edinburgh at Charlotte Square. Development had already begun north of the town, and the street running north (King Street as it became) was where the Trustees confidently expected new building to commence. It did not. One difficulty, which they might well have counted on, was a quibble with the Society of Advocates whose ground east of Lodge Walk marched with the west side of the new street: discussions over boundaries effectively neutralized that side of King Street until about 1815. Another and more serious difficulty was the standard of building suitable for the new streets—much bigger than anything built hitherto and consequently much dearer.

The trustees caused their supervisor, or architect as we would call him, Thomas Fletcher,[13] with James Burn,[14] to design a scheme in 1804, a composed terrace of the eighteenth century fashion, to encourage people to take up stances more readily (plate 9). The houses were of different widths, but they do compose: terminal blocks, one at either end, and with a block in the centre, give some sense of the magnificence that Young had proposed. The terrace was begun in 1805 with 8-10 King Street: it was not until 1810 that the rest of the southern end was built, Brebner's Block at the corner with the Castlegate, and 12-14 King Street, both by John Smith (who had succeeded Thomas Fletcher in 1807). Over the years the rest of the terrace was finished to Fletcher's and Burn's design with one very notable exception. The episcopalians in Aberdeen secured the important centre stances, but instead of building a suite of three houses with a pediment featured in the centre, they built a Perpendicular Gothic style chapel, and in sandstone! Perhaps sensing the bankruptcy which in fact came the next year the trustees were so addled that they agreed to such an extra-ordinary departure from their design—simply to secure the bargain.

The west side of King Street, with minor adjustments, was to follow the same design. In 1818 Archibald Simpson[15] began the Surgeon's Hall in the middle of the site opposite the chapel in a sober Greek revival style with four free standing columns supporting a porch, all of the Ionic Order. But even so, it was only two stories high instead of the required form, and to give their hall sufficient prominence the Medico-Chirugical Society got the trustees to vary the feu charter for the stances to either side so that future building on them would have to be set back. What might well have been stylistic disaster was turned to triumph by the skills of Smith, Simpson and Gillespie Graham, who between them built the west side of King Street from 1818 to 1840, working contrapuntally: Smith responded to the 'problem' posed by the Surgeon's Hall by at once making his building (for the Record Office) individual and at the same time fit in to Simpson's design so as to appear almost part-fit; then Smith's North Church of 1829, terminating the north end of the 'terrace', is recalled first by Graham's pedimented block of 1836 at 6-8 King Street, and finally in 1839 by Simpson at the Clydesdale Bank.[16]

The picturesque quality of the composition of the west side of King Street was recognised in Thomas MacKenzie's drawing of it. But one suspects it is picturesque rather more by accident than by conscious art of the designers. However that may have been, exploitation of picturesque possibilities, and the employment of historically allusive features in building, became characteristic in Aberdeen from about 1840. This we can trace back to the eighteenth century. Kames had gone on to amplify his rather conventional remarks about architecture by adding a genuinely revolutionary notion: 'architecture and gardening cannot otherwise entertain the mind than by raising certain agreeable emotions or feelings.[17] In other words, there was an association of ideas established in environmental arts. It was not enough to be simple, unaffected (or alternatively magnificent), and appropriate. There had to be—or there might be—something else. There might be an architectural form appropriate to a particular place, or mood, or function—a building might speak of its special nature. For a prison, such as Aberdeen's Bridewell, the castle style might be appropriate: it was forbidding in its bulk and obviously strong and yet it was venerable also, like the law. James Burn's prison stood athwart what is now Rose Street from 1809 to 1869. Its existence spans the transition from classic to Caledonian and it doubtless played a role in that change of taste.

Obviously, churches also might have some historical

relevance, as we have seen with Simpson and St Andrew's, and as we see with Smith at the South Church (plate 11)—one of a trio of churches with St Clements and Nigg, all more or less to the same design, and all suggesting a kinship with the sixteenth century and a rather vague, perhaps Tudor, quality. Sometimes these ideas, these relationships, could go quite far afield. I do not think Simpson actually knew Marburg in Germany but the two spires on the Elizabethkirke of the thirteenth century are very like our own magnificent, and still standing, despite scandalous neglect, Triple Kirks spire.

The association of ideas as aesthetic system developed in parallel with the English Landscape Garden, and from the 1780s the two became united in the cult of the picturesque, so that as well as alluding to history, a place or a mood, buildings could take their forms from romantic painted scenes. Simpson, James Souttar[18] and other architects recognised the picturesque qualities of the back of Belmont Street and their buildings there reflect this sensitivity. As the century goes on these linked ideas developed. Thus it is easy to see the appeal of old collegiate buildings such as King's College. In 1822, when Smith was called in to do something with it, King's College was in a very romantic and mouldering condition. There had been mar-vellous designs to make it smart, regular and classical to suit the eighteenth century taste, but despite his attempts to make Aberdeen conform to these ideals Smith responded fully to the college's charm.

As early as 1815 John Smith had worked on a romantic, picturesque house in the castle style for Lord Forbes.[19] Castle Forbes, near Alford, is an asymmetrical composition of indi-vidual strong forms about a prominent round tower at the junction of the two main fronts, and as such can trace its lineage through John Nash at Blaise near Bristol, or Conkhill (Shropshire), back to Doniston, the Welsh Borders romantic castle built by one of the principal exponents of the picturesque, Richard Payne Knight. Castle Forbes owed something to its place as well; not only the rough dressed granite, but perhaps there is an allusion to Towie Barclay in the south-west pavilion.

Modern castles had been built in Scotland from the mid 1740s (and indeed some had only left off the old fashion a couple of generations before that) but they had been regular, that is, symmetrical compositions, and they often appear as if castle-like ornaments and form were substituted for Palladian ones without actually altering the underlying design. The inclination to make new or remodelled castles symmetrical must have been a very strong one for both landowners and their architects. At Cluny, near Monymusk, for example there were a variety of schemes produced from the 1790s to modernize the old tower house. All ignored the essentially asymmetrical nature of the Z-plan and all attempted to regularize the scheme. In the event it was John Smith's design that was built and which caused James Skene of Rubislaw to write that 'a huge mushroom cotton manufactory has been raised up by the proprietor of this beautiful and antique gem'.[20]

Smith did not always treat castles in such a cavalier fashion; indeed, he could be remarkably gentle and self effacing. At Craigievar he repaired, he modernised to a degree (for instance, he installed sash windows), but mostly he nurtured what he found, and it is to him that we owe its survival. Known as 'Tudor Johnnie', Smith seems to have made a speciality of the castle style, and by the 1830s he had perfected J.C. Loudon's prescription of the 'Turret Style'[21] into something more genuinely local. Easter Skene House of 1832 has the turrets, the high roofs, Tudor windows, dormers and arrow slots as well as the essential informal composition.

It is easy to appreciate the appeal of a revived Scots Baronial style for country houses, and from the 1840s it becomes typical. But the use of romantic and asymmetrical buildings in Aberdeen could have been disastrous. Indeed, it ought to have been disastrous. Why was it not? Any change in mood or style can be borne if it does not happen too quickly, and if it respects what has gone before. And when the Scots Baronial came to town in Aberdeen it was used, initially, to reinforce qualities of the picturesque, and to underline the antiquity of the institutions which commissioned the buildings.

The first non-classical building in Union Street[22] was John Smith's Trinity Hall (plate 12). Built for the Seven Incorporated Trades, its turrets and Tudor details suggested a building of the period of their old hall in Guild Street, that is, late sixteenth century. In terms of mass, material and general form, Smith's building balanced Archibald Simpson's regular Aberdeen Hotel which had occupied the opposite site since the 1820s. Even so, its effect must have been extraordinary, especially as both buildings terminated the ranges of Union Street at Union Bridge, and were seen not only at a distance—from the bridge itself, from Union Terrace, or from Windmill Brae—but from a number of different angles. Hence Smith's use of a sixteenth century style enhances the inherent picturesque character of his site, just as we have seen Simpson had done two years previously at the Triple Kirks site. Similarly St John's Episcopal Church takes advantage of its prominent site (opposite and to the south of Trinity Hall) to display itself as a picturesque composition in a curiously English style.

Christ's College is by the same architect, Thomas MacKenzie,[23] and was built a year later in 1850 (plate 13). It is a masterpiece of scenic design, for although it is symmetrical in iself, it is seen from Union Street at an angle so that with the tower to the rear the building appears correctly picturesque and pleasingly asymmetrical.[24] Without Christ's College, Union Street would be incomplete, or at least appear 'unfinished', but with its construction the whole enterprise is handsomely if surprisingly resolved.

MacKenzie's achievement was immediately seized upon by the granite merchant John Gibb in his proposal to build a grand public building of three stories at the east side of the Castlegate, and his design would have echoed Christ's College, and, as it were, formed its mirror image. Although Gibb's scheme is symmetrical, as was still thought proper for a civic structure, the prominent and decidedly off centre tower to the rear gave the whole composition the desired picturesque effect from the Castlegate itself, whereas from further away in Union Street the tower would have been as the axis.

The 1850s saw little building activity because of a slump, and Gibb's idea was not carried out until much later. But Peddie's and Kinnear's[25] winning entry in the competition for a new Town House on the north side of the Castlegate takes up the idea of the prominent asymmetrical tower, and from the late 1860s the effect from Union Street was nearly the same. In their civic architecture both Smith and MacKenzie, and Gibb as well, had avoided any specifically Scottish reference. Their details were Gothic of the Tudor period, for not only was

7. West St Nicholas Kirk, by James Gibbs, 1741; executed by James Wylie, 1752-55. (W. Brogden).

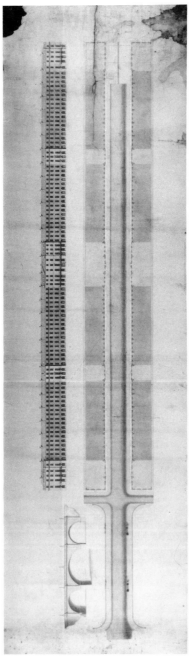

8. James Young, Design for the New Street, 1801. The only surviving drawing of the five competition entries for the 'New Streets of Aberdeen'. The extended palace block composition was to have stretched from the Castlegate to Union Bridge without a break. The idea owes much to Robert Adam's north side of Charlotte Square, Edinburgh of 1792: however, it predates the regular development of the second new town, and Percier and Fontaine's scheme for the Rue de Rivoli in Paris. (Aberdeen District Council).

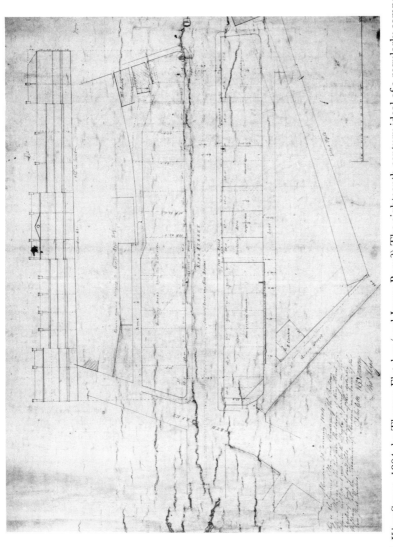

9. King Street, 1804, by Thomas Fletcher (and James Burn?) The eighteenth century ideal of a regularly composed terrace with pedimented centre piece, neutral terraced houses and high terminal blocks. (Aberdeen District Council).

10. King Street. Print showing its completion in 1840. The composition of buildings has become contrapuntal, if not picturesque. (Aberdeen City Library).

11. South Church, Belmont Street, by John Smith, 1830 (now known as St Nicholas Kirk House). (W. Brogden).

12. Trinity Hall, Union Street by John (and William) Smith, 1846. The hall was so much admired by the Prince Consort and the young Queen Victoria that the Smiths were commissioned to build Balmoral Castle. (W. Brogden).

13. Christ's College, Alford Place, by Thomas Mackenzie, 1850. The western termination to the classic Union Street, picturesque, alluding to (if not quite in) the Old Scotch Style. (Aberdeen City Library).

14. Rubislaw Terrace by Thomas MacKenzie, with James Giles consulting, carried on by James Matthews and others. Gables to front, with crowsteps, suggest old Scotland tempered by dormer from Renaissance France. Bay windows with plate glass are thoroughly modern 19th century. (W. Brogden).

the Perpendicular compositionally and structurally close to the
classic and therefore an easy and agreeable alternative, it also
possessed the necessary sense of history to give rise to an agreeable association of ideas, and it was picturesque. The Aberdonians, and other Scots, were slow to identify a civic Scottish
style as distinct from the perceived *national* British style, the vast
majority of whose monuments were located in England.

With Rubislaw Terrace, however, a specific Scottish quality
is brought to bear in urban design (plate 14). The terrace was
begun in 1852 by MacKenzie and his partner James Matthews[26]
though because of economic depression it was not finished until
the 1870s. The scheme was a private one for James Skene of
Rubislaw[27] who, with the artist James Giles as consultant, must
have encouraged the Scots features of the design, such as the
gables presented to the street front, a practice abandoned as
old fashioned and dangerous in the late seventeenth century.[28]
And the gables in Rubislaw Terrace are crow-stepped, as could
then still be seen on Skene's own ancient Rubislaw House.
There were also prominent dormers with architectural orna-
mentation in the style of Loire valley chateaux, and to roman-
tically inclined Aberdonians such a reminder of the Auld
Alliance was an agreeable one.

Throughout the 1850s there was the project to rebuild the
Grammar School. In view of its alleged antiquity a baronial
style would have been seen as appropriate. So it was, but not
initially, and not, apparently, without heated debate and soul
searching. A design exists, perhaps by Matthews, for a site on
Crown Terrace, near his partner's St Johns Episcopal Church,
and like it, placed so prominently on the bank of Windmill Brae
it would have had a picturesque effect, although its composition
and form are purely classical—presumably alluding to Latin
and classical culture, as the basis of the school's curriculum, as
having prior claims even to Scots Baronial.

A design competition was held in 1857 but the results by
George Smith of Edinburgh and James Matthews were dis-
missed as 'only two sets of mediocre drawings which a city
architect could have produced at a tithe of that money'.[29] Apart
from their 'mediocrity' we know nothing of these designs. By
1861 Matthews had produced his Scots Baronial design for a
practically rural site on the Denburn. Perhaps it is because of

the openness of the situation that the Grammar School was more extensive, even rambling, than a more urban site would have allowed, and its picturesque qualities are achieved by playful massing of elements within the building itself to be appreciated serially, rather than as a set piece object to be viewed at a distance. Therefore the Grammar School is more like a country house in its composition, and it is frankly Scottish in its detail—crow step gables, decorated dormer heads, turrets of various kinds, and a prominent square tower with a caphouse which in turn carries a turret.

With Union Street nearly complete, Aberdeen began to address persistent problems of areas of obvious degredation, where slums had increased with the quite remarkable growth of Aberdeen from a provincial town to a city of empire, and whose miserable aspect the brilliant white granite of the newer buildings only made worse. In the old town—near the Green and Windmill Brae, and to the south and east at the Shiprow, parts of Broad Street, but particularly the Gallowgate—great areas were overcrowded, insanitary and unsafe. To the north of Union Bridge, and in full view, was the industrial mess of Gilcomston—low, mean, dirty, and old without even the saving grace of appearing venerable. These problems the good Victorians of Aberdeen began to sort out in the 1880s, and with characteristic will, led by James Matthews, by now provost.

The scheme which was concocted was as bold and visionary, and as difficult to perform, as the King Street/Union Street scheme had been. By viaducts, embankment, and prodigiously high buildings yet another new street was envisaged—to run from the end of Schoolhill at the Triple Kirks, over the Denburn, masking Gilcomston with embankment, then over the Denburn again at Jock's Brae and hence up the long slope to Rosemount. And from Schoolhill eastward the Upperkirkgate was to be remodelled and lead finally to the heart of the city at Marischal College. In these new improvements Aberdeen learned from the early nineteenth century projects, avoiding delays and false starts, and the whole scheme was virtually complete within ten years. The town also learned how to turn an awkward and almost insoluable problem to advantage by perceiving that the town itself, or certainly significant sections of it, could be treated like a large and

15. The eastern termination of Union Street. On axis is the Salvation Army Citadel of 1893-6 by James Souttar. The tower, quoted directly from Balmoral, was apparently insisted upon by General Booth himself. (W. Brogden).

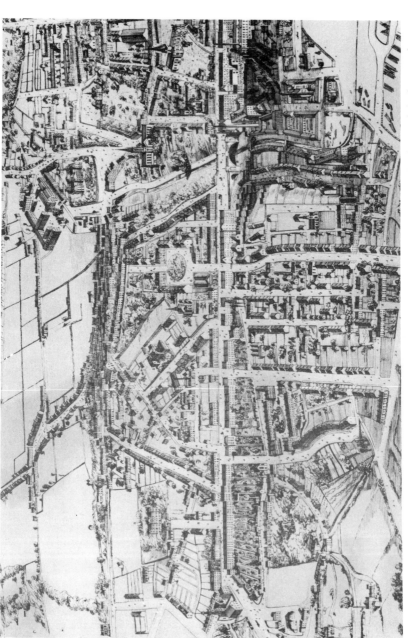

16. Aberdeen in 1850 shown in the bird's-eye drawing by George Washington Wilson. To the south is the grand, new and wide street, carried on vaults, causeways and bridges, while to the north the still medieval jumble of Broad Street, Netherkirkgate and Schoolhill can be seen: westward is Gilcomston straddling the Denburn, with Rosemount in its suburban state. (Aberdeen University Press).

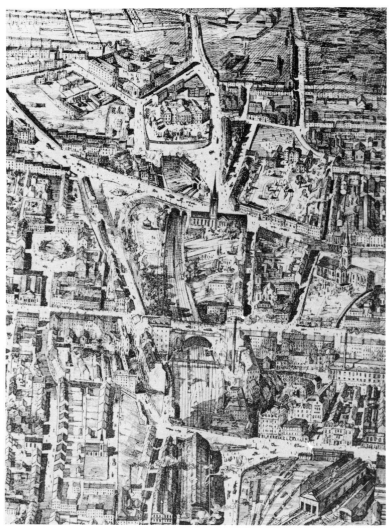

17. Aberdeen in 1889. George Washington Wilson's second, and better known, bird's-eye drawing. The Denburn and Rosemount Viaducts have been built, as has part of the Library, and St Mark's Kirk. By the end of the century the scheme had been largely completed. (Aberdeen District Council).

18, 19. Upperkirkgate. New buildings from the 1880s mixed with the old.
(W. Brogden).

19.

20. 6 Upperkirkgate by R.G. Wilson, 1899. Homage to Scottish architectural heritage. (W. Brogden).

21. 24-26 Upperkirkgate, 1694 (restored). The large bracket-like lugs at the top corners are original, as are their sundials: an open gallery was built between them. (W. Brogden).

22. Schoolhill and Upperkirkgate in 1988. Marshall MacKenzie's 'new' towers were always the picturesque termination; John Rust's pub at 1 George
Street took up the idea and added the turret. (W. Brogden).

LOOKING DOWN SCHOOLHILL TO UPPERKIRKGATE, ABERDEEN.   14,542.   G.W.W.

23. The same view in the early 20th century. (George Washington Wilson Collection, University of Aberdeen).

picturesque object such as the Grammar School, and like that building (or the larger modern castles) the town is seen serially, that is, one thing after another. Instead of suppressing this fact, as the Georgians had done by repetition of identical elements, rather the changes could be exploited by ornamenting them freely with both classic and Caledonian elements. Furthermore the contrast between this curving and changeful new street from Rosemount to Marischal College and the grand and straight Union Street was agreeable in itself.

The new street has three zones: the Upperkirkgate within the old town (plates 18-29), a civic group in the middle at the Denburn (plates 30-2), and the Rosemount Viaduct tenements (plate 34). Two and three storey blocks of tenements had been built in Rosemount from the 1870s, but the blocks on either side of the Viaduct were to be much bigger, five or six stories high above the pavement (and as many as three below) and built as five big blocks or terraces.[30] These contained flats for rent, self contained and thus private, of usually three to four rooms, and they provided decent and modern accommodation for families of moderate to slim means. 96-120 Rosemount Viaduct, built by James Souttar in 1887, is enlivened by turrets (originally they had peaked witches' hat roofs) crow step gables, and Gothic tracery, but there are pillars between windows as singles or pairs, suggesting an underlying classic order to the Caledonian block. Alexander MacKay's blocks, also of 1887, are more like conventional tenements, and their ornamented roofscape is less overtly Scottish but just as picturesque. The last block, by Brown and Watt and built ten years later, presents a concave frontage, and its sharp tower-like ends (made into oriel windows in the flats) are emphasised.

These blocks of tenement flats, with plate glass fronted shops at ground floor level, created an inhabited wall, richly ornamented and appropriately civic to connect, literally and metaphorically Union Terrace, Skene Street, Rosemount and Schoolhill.

Between the two viaducts the Denburn valley was artificially embanked to form the Union Terrace Gardens, and on the mound at the north end is the group of more civic buildings— the library, St Marks Church (sporting not only full classical portico, but a high drum and dome as well) and the theatre— all guarded by the giant statue of William Wallace. Viewed from Union Bridge on the Gardens this is a handsome and picturesque group, but equally it provided the heart of the new improvements, a centrepiece from which Union Bridge and Union Terrace could be appreciated, but from which Belmont Street and the old town could be seen to picturesque effect, especially as Rosemount Viaduct turns towards Aberdeen in a gentle curve.

In the third section of the new improvements another group of civic buildings was formed about a 'square' at the end of Schoolhill (plates 26-9). Fomerly the site of the Grammar School the space was retained and its north and east edges were built up by A. Marshall MacKenzie as the Art Gallery and Gray's School of Art while the south side was occupied by Ogg Allan's Central School. The west side was open to the Viaducts, and used Simpson's existing Triple Kirks as a picturesque foil. From Schoolhill to Marischal College the Upperkirkgate was retained, with new buildings added, such as John Rust's pub at 1 George Street, built as a public bar, contributing a most valuable turret to the scene, or R.G. Wilson's somewhat more scholarly homage to Scottish architectural heritage at 6 Upperkirkgate.

However, the new improvements were not achieved without bruising, indeed grieviously wounding, Aberdeen and cherished relics of its glorious past. Imagine a project which included the destruction of King's College Chapel *and* Provost Skene's House: to us in the late twentieth century such vandalism seems so monstrous as to be impossible. But a hundred years ago Victorians were almost giddy with success in nearly every field, and although they had learned to value Scots Baronial for its associational and picturesque qualities, that valuation did not extend to valuing the mouldering old buildings themselves: it was only the enlightened few who lamented their destruction. So Mar's Castle and Jamieson's House[31] were swept away, quite needlessly. Their destruction saw the beginnings of a conservationist attitude, particularly with the builder John Morgan and many of the architects, but it has taken a very long time to convince Aberdonians that the conservationists are right.

Aberdonians then, and subsequently too, like Matthews and A. Marshall MacKenzie[32] were convinced that the bright, new

24. Schoolhill, looking west, in 1988. Model tenements on the north side were built by Provost James Matthews' firm and replaced the house of the seventeenth century portrait painter George Jamieson. (W. Brogden).

25. Schoolhill. Shirras Laing's by James Rust 1887. A freer, more rectilinear but still allusively Scottish block. The tower to the right is one of four on Gibson and Pacitti's new Clarke Building for Robert Gordon's Institute of Technology. (W. Brogden).

26, 27. Schoolhill. This short section with the 'square' in front of Robert Gordon's Institute of Technology and the Art Gallery (28, 29) formed the transition between medieval Aberdeen (recalled by Greyfriars Kirk tower) and the Viaducts and Rosemount. (W. Brogden).

27.

28, 29. Schoolhill 'square'. At this angle Peddie and Kinnear's new Town House Tower of 1868-74 has become the termination. (W. Brogden).

29.

30, 31. Denburn Viaduct. Although derived from mostly classical sources the elements are displayed to advantage from numerous angles: the composition is picturesque and at the same time suggests a Kamesean association of ideas. (W. Brogden).

31.

32. Union Terrace and Skene Street. Domes (for learning and the classical past) and spires (for religion and gothic antiquity) in a free picturesque composition, echoed by the tenement blocks of Rosemount Viaduct. (W. Brogden).

33. Union Terrace and Skene Street.

34. 96-120 Rosemount Viaduct. Tenement flats over shops by James Souttar, 1887. The Old Scotch Style, with some gothic ornament, applied to ordinary dwellings. (W. Brogden).

35. Crown Street, GPO by W.T. Oldreive, 1907. The Old Scotch Style made official. The short section of Crown Street south of Union Street was rebuilt at the beginning of the twentieth century. The classic houses were replaced by buildings in a variety of freer styles, but the GPO employed Scots Baronial in a scholarly, and scenographically ingenious manner. However, the style's appeal died with Queen Victoria. (W. Brogden).

replacements were obviously to be preferred. So despite having prepared designs to retain Old Greyfriars Kirk, predating Marischal College itself and always its chapel, in the end the university and civic authorities had Marshall MacKenzie sweep it away in favour of his design for a brand new frontage to Broad Street which included a new Greyfriars Kirk. It must be admitted that Marischal College does give a most suitable termination to Aberdeen's second big nineteenth century project. Its clustered towers are especially effective when seen from Schoolhill, even now, after the further and less skilful intervention of the St Nicholas Centre. But once Broad Street is reached the towers of Marischal College are much less prominent and the texture of its long frontage is more apparent; most apparent is the tower of the Town House at the corner of Broad Street and the Castlegate.

Which brings us back to the beginning. In 1893 James Souttar finally realised the project for a big picturesque building to close the east side of the Castlegate. The Salvation Army Citadel, apparently on instruction from General Booth himself, quotes the tall square tower of Balmoral, and presents it to Aberdeen as a splendid termination to both the classically conceived Union Street and the Caledonian inspired new improvements.

Scots Baronial is practically contemporary with Queen Victoria. Although the General Post Office in Crown Street (plate 35) signals the 'official recognition' of the style, already architectural design had moved in quite different directions. The free playing with elements which characterizes Edwardian design allowed for the incident, interest and individuality which originally attracted Aberdonians to the Old Scotch Style, but the bombastic Imperial had little effect on the city. By 1914 Aberdeen was complete as an act of civic design. The twentieth century is another, sadder, story.

REFERENCES

1.   Two recent examples will illustrate this point: R. Dixon's and S. Muthesias' *Victorian architecture* (London, 1985), 170, gives only a few lines to the Scottish Baronial as just 'another medievalizing style'; and Mid-

dleton and D. Watkin in *Neoclassical and nineteenth century architecture* (part of a magisterial survey of world architecture: Milan and London, 1980), ii, 357, refer to the style indirectly as a spur to Viollet-le-Duc's emperial client Louis-Napoleon—somewhat misleadingly from the geographical point of view: 'in April 1855 the emperor and empress travelled to England. They did not see Balmoral Castle, then barely complete, but they returned determined to emulate it'.

2. Archibald Simpson (1790-1847), one of the principal architects in the breathtaking expansion of the city in the early nineteenth century. His work in Aberdeen is (with significant exceptions) characterised by an almost monumental sobriety allied to a scholarly sense of precedent. For Simpson, and for the architecture of Aberdeen generally see my *Aberdeen. An illustrated architectural guide* (Edinburgh, 1986).

3. Ionic, the middle of the architectural orders, (between Doric and Corinthian) first perfected in ancient Greece, characterized by a slenderness of members and the memorable volutes of the capitals.

4. Henry Home, Lord Kames (1696-1782) author of the popular and influential *Elements of criticism* (Edinburgh, 1762).

5. James Gibbs (1682-1754) born in Aberdeen and doubtless the greatest architect the city has produced. But he trained in Rome and practised in England, where his most famous building is St Martins in the Field, London. West St Nicholas is one of only two Gibbs' buildings in Scotland.

6. James Wyllie, an Edinburgh mason.

7. William Law, a builder-architect, responsible with Littlejohn and William Smith, elder for eighteenth century expansion and improvement in the town, generally in Broad Street, Queen Street, Littlejohn Street and other subsequently demolished streets on the then north-eastern edges of the town. For Aberdeen in the eighteenth century see my 'The architecture of eighteenth century Aberdeen' in Jennifer Carter and Joan Pittock-Weston (eds.), *Aberdeen and the Enlightenment* (Aberdeen, 1987).

8. Tenements were divided into parts or 'holdings'. For eighteenth century Aberdeen such a holding was a room, or set of rooms without any sense of completeness or privacy. From the end of the century they became tenement flats and self-contained. As the nineteenth century progresses their form becomes more set until the 1880s sees the typical Aberdeen type.

9. William Dauney, architect of Provost Young's House, 30 Marischal Street, and uncle to Archibald Simpson.

10. William Smith, elder. Builder/architect in Aberdeen; father of the famous John and grandfather of William, younger (architect of Balmoral) and John, younger. Some of the elder William Smith's work survives in the houses of lower Marischal Street.

11. John Smith (1781-1852), like the other great early nineteenth century Aberdeen architect, Simpson, began by employing classic styles. But his interest in classicism was neither so scholarly nor so monumental as Simpson's, and from an early stage he began to become interested as much if not more in the picturesque and associational qualities of Tudor or old Scottish buildings.

12. Charles Abercrombie, an engineer engaged on the turnpike roads in Kincardineshire and Aberdeenshire, and also involved with the Aberdeenshire Canal which ran from Waterloo Quay in the Harbour to Inverurie. In his *Further improvements* published at the beginning of the nineteenth century Abercrombie proposed a regular series of streets, squares and crescents beyond the Denburn, as well as Union Street and King Street.

13. Thomas Fletcher, an engineer principally, was also the assistant to the Trustees for the New Streets and in a sense the first city architect, although that honour is generally accorded to his successor John Smith. Fletcher left Aberdeen in 1807 for more interesting jobs, just before actual building in earnest began.

14. James Burn, of Haddington, where most of his practice was concentrated from 1777 to the early 1820s. The Bank of Scotland and the original Athenaeum next door are his most notable contributions to Aberdeen.

15. Smith had just replaced Simpson at Castle Forbes—see n.19 below.

16. The Clydesdale Bank took the place of the New Inn, a mid eighteenth century building.

17. Henry Home, Lord Kames *Elements of criticism*. For a fuller discussion of the aesthetics of association of ideas see J.M. Crook, *The dilemma of style* (London, 1987), 17.

18. James Souttar, architect with William Leslie of the Congregational Church in Belmont Street. This building, although basically a plain box, presents its liurgical 'east' end to the neo-classical Aberdeen of Union Terrace as a quotation of the east end of the Romaneque cathedral of Lund, which Souttar knew from his years in Stockholm (1863-5). William Leslie (1802-79) built Dunrobin Castle in Sutherland from 1844, and although Sir Charles Barry was its architect he credited Leslie with the planning and execution of extensions 'in the grand and picturesque style of architecture peculiar to Scottish Castles' see *Aberdeen. An illustrated architectural guide*, 33.

19. Castle Forbes had been Archibald Simpson's commission, his first in independent practice, in 1814. Perhaps because of his inexperience the original house, called Putachie, which it was intended to keep as a feature of the new building, was undermined and had to be demolished. Smith was called in to finish the job. The full story is fully and wittily told in J. Macaulay *The Gothic Revival 1745-1845* (London, 1975), 205-8.

20. Quoted by Harry Gordon Slade in his thorough account of 'Cluny Castle, Aberdeenshire' in *Proceedings of the Society of Antiquaries of Scotland*, 111 (1981), 454.

21. J.C. Loudon, *Treatise on forming, improving and managing country residences* (London, 1806), 111-13. This is the earliest reference to what we call Scots Baronial, and Loudon's characterization of the style is typically complete. His suggestion that 'New styles of considerable beauty may be formed by inventing new modes of finishing parapets...' (112) is prophetic.

22. The only other non-classical buildings in the street are Langstane and Gilcomston South Kirks. There was formerly a rather impudent bank in Perpendicular Gothic form at the corner of St Nicholas Street, built in the 1880s, but it was replaced in 1936 by the classical Royal Bank of Scotland.

23. Thomas MacKenzie (1815-1854). The very gifted and too short lived begetter of the great architectural dynasty whose best monument is Marischal College. MacKenzie worked with both Smith and Simpson, and indeed it may well have been MacKenzie himself who worked up the pleasingly Tudor designs for Marischal College which Simpson was engaged on in the late 1830s. Thomas MacKenzie moved to Elgin in 1841, and his practice in Aberdeen was carried on with his former assistant James Matthews.

24. MacKenzie appears to have had two purposes, to make the tower appear axially to Union Street, that is, in the centre of the otherwise empty space at the west end: and to have the whole appear picturesque. So he placed the tower at the extreme right end of Christ's College, and because of the angle of the building it would appear to be nearer the centre, and to preserve the effect of the picturesque the secondary tower carrying the stair was placed at a corner of the main tower.

25. J.D. Peddie (1824-91) and C.G.H. Kinnear (1830-94) won the commission for the new Town House in Aberdeen by anonymous competition early in their partnership, and its success was the basis of their subsequent practice.

26. James Matthews (1820-1898), in partnership with Thomas MacKenzie 1844-1854, had previously worked in London with George Gilbert Scott. Thomas MacKenzie's more famous son, A. Marshall MacKenzie, was first a pupil of James Matthews and subsequently his partner. With Matthews' growing interest in political affairs in the 1880s, and especially in the improvements which resulted in the Denburn and Rosemount Viaducts and the associated clearance of slums, he effectively withdrew from practice.

27. James Skene of Rubislaw. A private improver. Skene was responsible for carrying on the ideals of regular and grand expansion begun by Abercrombie and carried on, sometimes fitfully, by Simpson, Smith and

others. As early as 1819 Skene commissioned a regular 'newtown' on his property the Damlands—now the West End of Aberdeen. Simpson began building there to a different design, which was again modified by Matthews as his successor. But Skene was also a considerable anti-quarian with a genuine and pioneering taste for Scottish Baronial (see for example Slade, 'Cluny Castle, Aberdeenshire', 483) so that by 1852 when Rubislaw Terrace was begun these tastes, with the general tend-ency of architecture at the time, played their part in the terraces' significant move towards the Caledonian.

28. The only surviving building with a gable to the street can be seen in the Upperkirkgate at number 42.

29. *Building Chronicle*, June 1857 quoted in *Aberdeen, An illustrated architectural guide*, 104.

30. A sixth block, Rosemount Square, was added between 1938 and 1946.

31. Mar's Castle stood on the Gallowgate near the present Seamount Flats. Dating from the sixteenth century it presented turrets and gables plus venerable age. These qualities did not outweight its ruinous and dis-gusting state as a slum, but its destruction still caused controversy. The destruction of Jamieson's House caused a furore: a cartoon appeared in the *Bon-Accord Magazine* (reproduced in *Aberdeen. An illustrated architectural guide*, 26) showing the 'modern vandals at work', for not only was Jamieson's House 'a good example of Scotch turreted work', it was also the home of Scotland's most famous painter of the seventeenth century. Its removal really was a shocking and stupid act, but lord provosts will not be told, even if they had been architects of skill such as James Matthews.

32. Alexander Marshall MacKenzie (1848-1933), son of Thomas MacK-enzie, practised with Matthews from 1877 to 1893, and thereafter on his own account.

ABERDEEN HARBOUR—THE TAMING
OF THE DEE

John S. Smith

The River Dee enters the North Sea at a point where the character of the coastline changes dramatically. The rocky promontory of Girdleness forms the southern end of the sandy arc of Aberdeen Bay. The exit channel of the river has been maintained on the southern flank of Aberdeen Bay by the continuing accumulation of sediment trapped against the flanks of Girdleness. The net accumulation of sediment resulting from the activities of waves driven by north-easterly winds operating across a lengthy sea fetch narrowed the entrance to the original Dee estuary, and maintained the exit channel hard by the Torry shore. The Sandness peninsula, clearly highlighted on both James Gordon's 1661 map and John Slezer's engraving of c.1696 was the main surface manifestation of these physical processes of sediment movement in a southerly direction. In addition the river entry to the bay was further impeded by a submerged sandbar whose presence Gordon draws attention to in his 'Description of both Touns'. The Dee decanted much of its sediment load into the large embayment behind the Sandness, particularly during spring tides when the river was ponded upstream at the top of the tide. Further complements of sediment were supplied by the small burns which drained the hollows between the gravel 'hills' on which the burgh of Aberdeen was then concentrated. The original embayment or estuary extended westwards to below Ferryhill, then swung north-eastwards to wash the foot of the Shiprow, St. Katharine's Hill and the Castlehill, thence southwards along the flanks of the Sandness. Within the estuary thus defined a myriad of channels and 'inches' developed, often changing their positions as a result of the changing energies of river and tide, and creating a dynamic environment of channel plan and depth inappropriate to easy access by even the smallest trading vessels. The Gordon map gives a clear picture of the Dee estuary in its near-natural state: cluttered by mud and sandbanks which dried out at low tide, but also characterised by more permanent inches with salmon fishers' huts which were awash at spring tides. The impression is of very shallow water although a deeper channel is shown on the northern flank—running from the entry of the Den Burn towards Pocra and hugging the north shore— ultimately joining the main Dee channel off Torry on the southern margin of the estuary. The ships of the day lay off Torry or off Futty, and from there passengers and cargo were taken ashore in smaller boats. Only at the highest tides could the smallest traders reach the townhead quay. For perspective it is important to remember that throughout the seventeenth century the average cargo seldom reached forty tons.

The stimulus to improve the estuary for trading vessels came in part through a general deterioration in the entrance to the haven during the late seventeenth century. A government surveyor engaged to make a survey of all Scottish ports reported that, in Aberdeen's case, sand driven in by wave activity had through shallowing 'rendered the estuary lesse usefull of late than formerly' while another visitor neatly summed up the difficult physical environment of the Dee estuary by observing that 'a stranger could never find the port as he left it'. The basic physical problems of inadequate water depth both within and at the entrance to the Dee estuary were the twin characteristics which were tackled during the eighteenth and nineteenth centuries, with attention initially concentrated on the imbalance between the potential scouring activities of Dee-derived water, and the large quantities of sediment transported southwards along the then dune-fringed beach of Aberdeen Bay. A series of rather piecemeal efforts to tackle the problems in the late seventeenth and the eighteenth centuries had limited success, with the main breakthrough taking place in the nineteenth century. It was during that century that the basis of the present harbour layout was established through the efforts of a succession of prominent civil engineers.

The difficult physical situation in the estuary had already been recognised in the eighteenth century and certain works,

notably a North Pier running out from the Sandness along the
northern side of the entrance channel for 300 yards had been
constructed on the advice of John Smeaton in 1770. The effects
were to check the ingress of sand and to change slightly the
angle of incoming waves at the entrance. The entrance bar
shifted from its original position into rather deeper water. The
overall gain was some three to four feet of water depth. By
1778 a follow-up survey by Smeaton recognised an unfortunate
knock-on effect of the 1770 improvements: 'the bold effects of
the sea running in along the pier wall caused too violent an
agitation in the harbour, proving inconvenient and dangerous'.
The construction of catch piers along the entrance channel
proved a satisfactory solution. On the basis of Smeaton's
reports, the perceived effects of the improvements of the 1770s,
and his own survey, Thomas Telford considered ways of making
major improvements to the interior parts of the estuary. His
Report on Aberdeen to the Lords of the Treasury dated 1801,
although short and forming part of a wider survey of the *Coasts
and Central Highlands of Scotland*, contained useful material relevant to the solution of the problem of developing the estuary
of the Dee for shipping. In contrasting the fall of the Dee and
Don, Telford noted that the former had little surface gradient
'for several miles back into the country' and that the tide flowed
inland for about two miles. He sketched the basic physical
geography of Aberdeen Bay noting the presence of a store of
loose sand from Collieston to Girdleness, with the Dee at the
southern end of the arc. He noted that strong north east winds
move sand southwards, but that the waters of the Dee 'especially
when augmented by land floods flow with much force and have
kept open a passage along the north side of the granite rocks',
this accumulation of sand forming the Sandness and also, within
the estuary, forming 'low ground of considerable width—
covered at high water—extends one mile up the Dee'. The
river course ran along the south side of this low ground, but in
floods, spilled to the north side forming 'a crooked channel'
upon the edge of which lay the town's quays. Here, as Telford
put it, 'vessels come in with the tides and transact their business'.
He calculated water depths over the entrance bar at ordinary
spring tides to be, at low water, little more than 'the run of the
river' and at neap tides, only ten feet—both these depths only

'at the very best state of the bar'. Thus with increasing port trade and larger vessels in use, the depth of water at the entrance tackled by Smeaton still remained 'a great inconvenience'.

Although Telford envisaged that improvements would be costly, he felt able to justify this on the grounds that Aberdeen 'is already a place of considerable trade, has many conveniences and accommodations, and abounds with enterprising and well-informed men'. His main proposals may be summarised as follows:

1. The securing and extending of the North Pier.
2. The adoption of a proper plan for managing the river, canal and entrance bar.
3. The improvement of the interior parts of the estuary.

Fortunately the City already had possession of sufficient ground for these purposes with the exception of the River Dee fisheries, which were in private hands. In April 1802, at the request of Aberdeen Town Council, Telford began the preparation of a plan for harbour development with the following aims:

a. The creation of the maximum extent of wharfage and wet docks for vessels to float at low tide.
b. The avoidance of damage to River Dee fisheries, but the acquisition of new ground for shipbuilding and rope making on the north side of the channel, and the provision of transport links to the new ground from the city.
c. The enhanced scouring of basins and the harbour entrance.
d. The achieving and maintaining of an additional four feet of water depth over the entrance bar, permitting the entry of naval ships and merchantmen at high water neaps.

The proposals when they emerged included a proper connection between the Aberdeen-Inverurie Canal and proposed wet dock. The estimated cost was given in 1802 at around £51,000, but a subsequent report dated 1809 revised the cost to £121,900.

The Telford scheme established the direction of improvements which were to continue right through the nineteenth century. Most of the proposals were pushed through via the acts of parliament of 1810, 1813 and 1829, although not without considerable controversy and local comment. The speed of implementation was held up by lack of available finance particularly in the period 1817-25. During the period up to the early 1840s the North Pier was extended, the South Breakwater constructed, and the Waterloo, Trinity and Regent Quays begun, together with deepening activities. The Wet Dock scheme was held up by lack of finance and by citizen objections largely relating to problems of sewage disposal. Only after the act of 1843 did work commence on the Victoria Dock and its lock entrance (1841-8)—appropriately completed in time for the royal yacht to berth in September 1848. For the first time in Aberdeen's history a stable water level within the dock allowed ships to lie alongside quays for goods to be unloaded by steam derrick, although distribution on land was initially by horse and cart. Further work took place on Blaikie's and Matthew's Quays. The sea lock for the Aberdeenshire Canal had been completed in 1834, but the bed became the property of the Great North of Scotland Railway in the early 1850s. The act of 1843 created a new governing body of Harbour Commissioners and they sold land in the inner part of the estuary to the Aberdeen Railway Company, who were at that time envisaging a railway terminus in the vicinity of the New Market.

In the second half of the nineteenth century the harbour works, which had been initially concentrated in the northern half of the estuary and at the entrance, gradually progressed southwards and it became increasingly clear that the waters of the Dee—seen by Smeaton, Telford and particularly by Rennie as a potential natural scouring agent for the harbour—were increasingly a hindrance to the realisation of the full potential of the estuary. The need for more quay space and for quayside land for processing and servicing industries associated with the port's growing trade encouraged a southern shift in investment emphasis, and only by realigning the Dee could this be satisfactorily achieved. By 1860 the first phase in the construction of Albert Quay was completed. The act of 1868 specified a further extension (the third) to the North Pier, the construction of a new re-sited South Breakwater (under way 1869-74) and permitted the diversion of the Dee, a task accomplished in 1871-3. The act of 1871 gave the Aberdeen Harbour Commissioners powers to purchase the Raik, Stell and Midchingle salmon

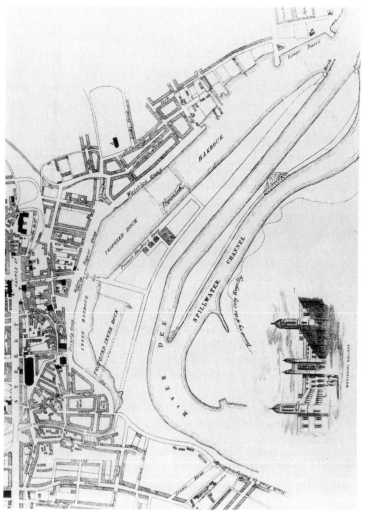

36. Nicol's map of Aberdeen Harbour (1840).

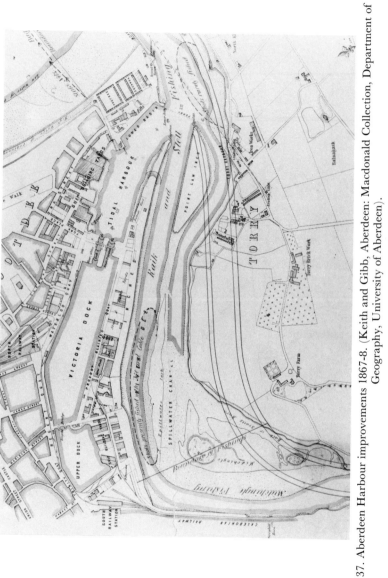

37. Aberdeen Harbour improvements 1867-8. (Keith and Gibb, Aberdeen: Macdonald Collection, Department of Geography, University of Aberdeen).

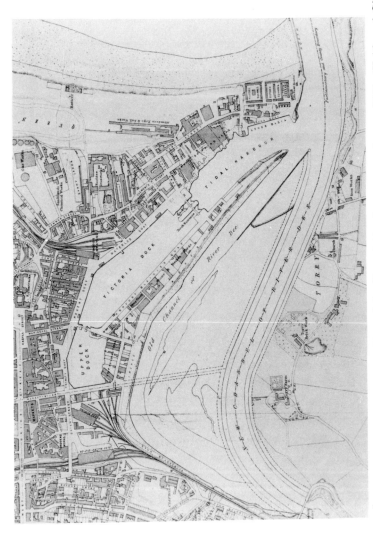

38. Aberdeen Harbour in 1871 (from a Plan of the City of Aberdeen corrected up to 1871. (Keith and Gibb, Aberdeen: Macdonald Collection, Department of Geography, University of Aberdeen).

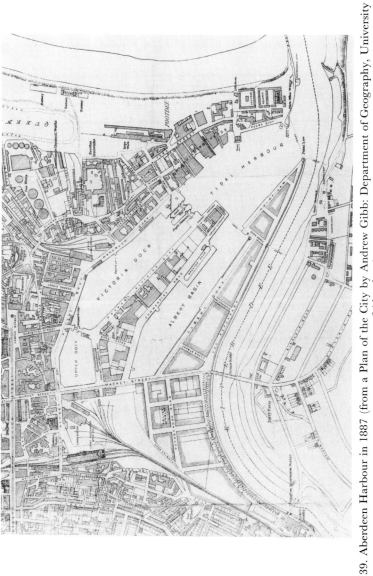

39. Aberdeen Harbour in 1887 (from a Plan of the City by Andrew Gibb: Department of Geography, University of Aberdeen).

fishings within the estuary together with the sea-netting rights from Broadhill to Girdleness—the sum of some £30,000 being paid in compensation. The cutting of the artificial channel for the Dee amply realised the demands for increased quay space in the Albert Basin (which broadly occupies the old channel of the river) and permitted the extension of Market Street southwards. The bridging of the Dee at the Victoria Bridge (1881) opened up fresh ground on the southern side of the estuary for both waterfront and residential development. The former Raik and Stell fisheries became the basis of the grid pattern of streets landward of the Albert Basin and Upper Dock.

The final phase of the North Pier was completed in the period 1874-9, Jameson's Quay was constructed, the Albert Quay extended, and the entrance lock to the Victoria Dock deepened. The increase in sea fish landings overwhelmed the temporary fish market on the Inches (on the west side of South Market Street adjoining the railway), and after considerable debate the Council decided on a new site at Commercial Quay West, completed in 1889, despite pleas from the Torry fishermen for a location on the southern side of the estuary. A process of eastward extension of fish landing space continued on into the twentieth century. At the very end of the nineteenth century (Harbour Acts of 1879 and 1887) the construction of Palmerston Quay and the Torry Harbour were under way.

The total nineteenth century package of improvements completed the modern outline of the harbour. The growing harbour trade envisaged by Telford in his initial 1801 survey justified the £1.5m spent on harbour improvements[1] between 1810 and 1872. The number of vessels using the port in 1799 was around 1,750 (total tonnage of 104,000), compared with 3,360 in 1899 (total tonnage of 956,000). Figures for vessel arrivals and departures categorised into foreign and coastwise trade are given below:[2]

	Vessel arrivals/departures in foreign trade	coastwise entries/ departures
1801	173	1,743
1875	320	1,489
1900	260	2,850
1960-1	559	1,786

40. Aberdeen Harbour from the Municipal Tower. The Victoria Dock is shown complete and the Albert Basin and Dee diversion is completed although there is considerable dredging activity off Footdee. (George Washington Wilson Collection, University of Aberdeen).

41. Aberdeen Harbour in the 1970s.

The development of the port provided the medium whereby the city developed its entrepot function for its region, channeling the flow of goods in and out of the North East. The coastal trade in coal of an annual 75,000 tons in the 1830s rose to 140,000 tons by 1850, and continued to grow despite competition from the railway. The chief foreign imports in the 1870s and 1880s of guano, sodium nitrate, linseed and esparto grass reflected the needs of the hinterland for fertiliser and livestock feed, and the demands of the suburban papermills. The chief exports over the same period were textiles, livestock, granite, paper and cereals. Despite being distant from the basic resources of coal and iron which fueled what one economic historian has termed the 'Scottish Victorian Economic Miracle',[3] Aberdeen contrived to treble its population between 1831 and 1901, while growth of population in its city region peaked as late as 1911. By comparison with its three Scottish rivals, Aberdeen was the most resilient of the Scottish cities, avoiding specialisation perhaps more by good luck than design. The creation of the harbour played a major role in this development of an adaptable economy. If the crossing of the Den Burn by Union Bridge and the construction of Union Street changed Aberdeen's image from a town to a city, so the taming of the Dee and its estuary created a port out of a haven.

APPENDIX: MAJOR NINETEENTH CENTURY IMPROVEMENTS TO ABERDEEN HARBOUR

1769	Consultation by Magistrates with Smeaton.
1780	Completion of first section of North Pier on Sandness. Improvement of entrance water depth resulted in increased trade.
1801-2	Consultation with Telford and reports/recommendations.
1810	Act of parliament permitting the implementation of certain of Telford's recommendations. This act also placed harbour affairs under Harbour Commissioners composed of Magistrates and Council. North Pier extended and Old South Breakwater constructed.

1829	Act of parliament obtained under which Harbour Board reconstituted by the addition of six members elected from the guildry and incorporated trades. Quays constructed included Trinity, Regent, and parts of Waterloo and Blaikie's Quays. Pocra Quay (1826-31), Old Regent Bridge (1832) and Regent Quay (completed in 1834) also constructed.
1843	Act of parliament empowering the Harbour Commissioners to proceed with a wet dock (the Victoria Dock) and the first Dock Gates (1844-8). Parts of Waterloo Quay, Blaikie's Quay and Matthew's Quay completed. Market Street was constructed in 1842.
1845	Aberdeen Railway Act passed—the intention being originally to run the line across Trinity Quay en route to a probable terminus at the New Market.
1848	On 7 September the royal yacht *Victoria and Albert* berthed in the Victoria Dock.
1868	Act of parliament including a further reconstitution of the Harbour Board into the form which continued on into the twentieth century. Under this act the North Pier was again extended and a new South Breakwater built, essentially replacing that of 1810. The navigation channel was improved, and approval obtained for the purchasing by the commissioners of the salmon fisheries. Certain sea-netting rights were also bought out. The diversion of the Dee into its present artificial channel between the Esplanade and Point Law was accomplished between 1870 and 1873, permitting extensive reclamation of the inches and feuing of this ground.
1871	Act of parliament including additional borrowing powers to buy out the salmon fishing interests.
1879, 1895	Acts of parliament permitting the construction of the Albert Basin, the deepening of the Victoria Dock entrance and the provision of new Dock Gates. In 1881, the Victoria Bridge was opened. Harbour Office built 1884. There was also construction of additional quays including some specifically designed for fish landings. 1889, new fish market at Commercial Quay completed, with a series of quay extensions which carried on into the twentieth century. Torry Harbour was completed in 1896.

BIBLIOGRAPHY

The main sources for the information contained in this paper are:

Harbour Commissioners, *An Act for Improving and Maintaining the Harbour of Aberdeen, 31 and 32 Vict, Cap. 138... with Clauses from other Acts incorporated therewith, or relating to the Harbour* (Aberdeen, 1869).

Harbour Commissioners, *Acts for Improving and Maintaining the Harbour of Aberdeen with Clauses from other Acts incorporated therewith, or relating to the Harbour* (Aberdeen, 1899).

Harbour Commissioners, *Aberdeen Harbour* (London, 1933).

Alexander Keith, *A Thousand Years of Aberdeen* (Aberdeen, 1972).

Andrew C. O'Dell, 'Transport of Aberdeen—The Port of Aberdeen', *Scottish Geographical Magazine*, 79 (1963), 108-113.

J.S. Smith, 'The Development of Aberdeen Harbour', *Aberdeen University Review*, 48 (1980), 391-403.

Thomas Telford, 'Mr Telford's Report of Aberdeen, made to Lords of the Treasury in 1801', *Fourth Report from the Committee of the Survey of the Coasts of Scotland—Naval Stations and Fisheries*, (1803), 100-4.

John R. Turner, *Scotland's North Sea Gateway. Aberdeen Harbour 1136-1986* (Aberdeen, 1986).

REFERENCES

1. A.C. O'Dell, 'Transport of Aberdeen', 110.
2. The decrease in vessel movements in the latter part of the nineteenth century was offset by substantial increases in the cargo capacity of individual ships.
3. S. and O. Checkland, *Industry and Ethos. Scotland 1832-1914* (London, 1984), 12.

THE DISRUPTION OF THE 'ESTABLISHMENT': JAMES ADAM AND THE ABERDEEN CLERGY

A. Allan MacLaren

On 18 May 1843 the Church of Scotland was torn apart by a schism of such magnitude that it was described as the Disruption. The wounds inflicted by the new Free Church on the Established Church were deep and long-lasting. The social consequences for Scottish society were immense but nowhere, as we shall see, were the immediate consequences for the Establishment as serious as they were in the city of Aberdeen. Within the Aberdeen social structure powerful groups were emerging who identified their interests with the need to make a success of the new Free Church. The destruction of the Church of Scotland was seen as a necessary part of this social process. The conflict inevitably produced heroes and villains on both sides, one man—James Adam, editor of the *Aberdeen Herald*—was to play a role which he never intended: although he consistently sought to undermine the morale and the intentions of the Aberdeen clergy considering schism, his influence on the scale of the crisis may well have been crucial.

The first part of this paper provides a general background to the Disruption in 1843; the next section examines the pattern of the secession in the city; the third section looks at the social consequences for Aberdeen society; finally the role of James Adam is considered.

General background to Disruption of 1843. Although the basic elements of the Disruption in the Church of Scotland can be

traced back to earlier secessions in the eighteenth century[1]—
the consequences of the Disruption were by far the more serious.
Ostensibly the issue was one of the patronage in the Church
whether a patron, or the kirk session and congregation, had the
right to present and confirm the minister of the parish. In reality
the issues ran much deeper than this and the issue of patronage
tended to polarise and provide a demarcation between two
distinct sections within the Church of Scotland. These sections
differed on far more than the rights of patrons. The struggle
between the Moderate and Evangelical parties became insti-
tutionalised into a debate over the rights to appoint ministers
but in effect it was what has been described as 'cleavage between
two incompatible philosophies of life'.[2] The Moderates were
more tolerant and permissive in their attitudes towards society
and certainly less puritanical with regard to their own behaviour. Culturally and socially they were more akin to the country
lairds to whom many in fact owed their appointment; theo-
logically they stressed 'mere morality', rejecting the fervent
enthusiasm and emphasis on hell-fire and predestination which
was so much part of their Evangelical counterparts. The Moderates were very much at home in polite society and under
their leadership the Church had become a more tolerant and
enlightened body which was closely associated with great
national and European cultural developments. On the other
hand their leadership had lost the Church about a quarter of
its membership to dissenting presbyterian denominations by
the end of the eighteenth century.[3] The Evangelicals—hardline
Calvinists in their attitude towards salvation and the need to
regulate society along clear Calvinist principles—underwent a
revival in the late eighteenth and early nineteenth centuries.
Their revival coincided with a period of rapid industrialisation
and urbanisation, population growth and migration; these
social and economic changes brought new problems for the
Church, particularly in terms of parochial organisation, poor
relief, and education.

In the 1830s the Evangelicals achieved a dominance in the
General Assembly and in the period known as the 'Ten Years
Conflict' successfully pushed through a series of Acts which
restricted the rights of patrons to 'intrude' their nominee. The
legality of these Acts was challenged in the House of Lords who

ruled against them. The issue now became a struggle between the State and the majority of the General Assembly who claimed the right of the Church to modify its own constitution without interference from the State. Neither side would concede and the Government of the time refused to intervene. In May 1843 the Disruption of the Church took place—about a third of the ministers seceding to form the Free Church.

Clerical and lay support for the schism came from two quite distinct social and geographical sources. Support was strong in the Highlands and Islands, where the Free Church to this day remains strongly entrenched, and overwhelming support for the new church can also be seen in the city parishes. In Glasgow twenty-five out of thirty-four ministers seceded; in Edinburgh twenty-four from thirty-five; in Dundee nine out of fourteen; and in Aberdeen all fifteen city ministers seceded.[4]

The secession in Aberdeen. Not surprisingly, the loss of all fifteen parishes devastated the Church of Scotland, which was left without a single minister to preach to its greatly depleted city congregations. If the Establishment was caught unprepared for this catastrophe it is clear that the seceders had begun planning at least seven months before the event. A remarkable fall in church collections took place as moneys were diverted into private funds to be used in the likelihood of future church building. Endowments were transferred and libraries removed for safe keeping. At communion in the East Parish in October 1842 it was ascertained what proportion of the male heads of families would secede. Collections were undertaken and commitments made which guaranteed the ministers' stipends in the event of secession. In one case the minister of the West Parish was assured of his stipend down to the last pinch of snuff as this was a small luxury of which he was particularly fond.[5]

As far as immediate church accommodation was concerned, arrangements were made to share premises with other dissenting denominations. In the case of one congregation a wooden church was erected and ready for the minister on his return from the Disruption assembly.[6] In the longer term, sites were obtained as close as possible to the Established churches so that the thinness of support for these churches could be clearly demonstrated. Strategy varied. Eight new sites were obtained and churches erected by March 1844 (West, South, East, Greyfriars, North, St. Clement's, Trinity, Gilcomston). In three cases the Establishment abandoned church and congregation (Melville, Mariners, Gaelic). In four cases the kirk sessions put the church building up for sale. Fear of undertaking payment of the debts on two of these churches meant that the seceders simply re-purchased the buildings, forcing the Establishment to abandon the charge (Union, Bonaccord). In the case of the other two (John Knox and Holburn) the Establishment fought their sale in court and succeeded in forcing the Free Church to build—which they proceeded to do.[7]

By 1851 when the *National Census of Religious Worship*[8] was carried out—the first and only government attempt to do so—it is clear that the Free Church in Aberdeen had established a remarkable numerical superiority in the city. It has been estimated that of those who attended church (28,423—38.59 per cent of the population) two-thirds were presbyterians. Out of the 386 in every 1,000 who attended church

> 162 belonged to the Free Church;
> 73 to the Church of Scotland;
> 52 were Episcopalian;
> 43 were Congregationalists;
> 27 were United Presbyterians;
> 12 were Roman Catholic;
>   7 were Methodists;

while remaining groups made up less than 5 per 1,000 each.

In 1843 the *Aberdeen Banner*—mouthpiece of the Free Church cause—had advocated a war against what it described as the 'Residuary Establishment'.

> It will be the policy of our enemies to do all they can to crush the rising Church ... we must carry on a war ... with all the force of a duty. We are not at liberty to do it, or not to do it ... [it is] an absurdity to imagine that we shall not aim at its destruction, and a sin to intend not to do so.[9]

By 1851 it was clear that this war had been fought and won. Certainly the Established Church had not been totally destroyed, but its survival in such a weakened state was a clear, if unnecessary, indicator of the comparative strength of the Free Church. The Church of Scotland had shrunk to nine congregations compared to the Free Church's fifteen. The fear obviously held in 1843 that the new church might become yet another 'puny Scotch sect' had long since vanished. The apprehension that secession might lead to a loss of social respect-ability—an anxiety felt by some seceding ministers—was never fulfilled. The fear was real enough, however, and there had been a general recognition by the seceders that 'comparability in all things' was the minimum that must be achieved in any comparative measurement of the two denominations. By 1851 the Free Church, certainly in Aberdeen, had emerged as a *new* 'Establishment'. The aim of comparability had been more than fully realised, but at a very considerable cost.

It is paradoxical that the same social forces which had been in the forefront in achieving the success of the Free Church also contained the seeds of that Church's subsequent problems. Whilst it would be wrong to underestimate the importance of the appeal to high-minded religious 'principles' in the secession, it would be equally mistaken to ignore the social forces which were generated from within the seceding congregations. The drive to secede—and succeed—came from dynamic sections of the Aberdeen middle class. These men were characterised by a high degree of social mobility based on a readiness to switch occupations and to diversify business interests. In their climb up the social ladder these same men might have made and unmade several business partnerships, and occupied any num-ber of business premises. But if their aggressive entrepreneurship in the field of business contrasted sharply with the staid respect-ability of their counterparts in the Church of Scotland eldership, so also were their lifestyles sharply differentiated. Whilst the adherents of the Established Church clung to the older resi-dential districts of the city around Castle Street, Adelphi, the east end of Union Street, the Upperkirkgate and the Nether-kirkgate, venturing as far as Belmont Street, the new men of the Free Church crossed over to the areas west of the Denburn, typically occupying several houses in a relatively short space of time in the new residential areas of Bonaccord Street, Crown Street, Dee Street, Union Place, Holburn Street, Carden Place, and Rubislaw.[10]

These were the men who alone had the dynamism, enterprise, organisational skills and wealth which were required to raise stipends to pay ministers, to find sites and finance for church building, and generally ensure the success of the Free Church which was clearly demonstrated by the census of religious worship in 1851. In their urgency and commitment by which they sought to ensure the success of the new church—they also sought to demonstrate their own abilities to the wider society. They left their mark on both.

Urged on to fight a war against what was described as the 'Residuary Establishment' in 1843 they fought the war utilising all their economic and financial expertise. It was self-evident that success meant harnessing all available financial resources, and in order to do this each church, each congregation, and ultimately each individual member, was regarded as part of a business enterprise. Contributions to church support schemes tended to become a measure of religious commitment of an individual. It tended also to become one of the more important criteria for election to eldership. Indeed in some kirk sessions where the pressure was great, it became a vital part of continued membership. In the bitter drive to destroy the old Establishment and become the new Free Establishment—comparability was sought in all things; thus we find Free Church buildings constructed as close as possible to the Established ones, and attempts as far as practicable to make the Free Church edifice more commodious and impressive to the eye. Free Church schools were constructed to rival Established ones. Philanthropic institutions were precisely duplicated, as were missions both at home and abroad. In seeking complete comparability with the Church of Scotland the Free Church did not destroy the Establishment, they simply became *another* Establishment. By becoming another Establishment (albeit without state support) they assumed all the financial difficulties of maintaining such a position. By creating a new Establishment, and all the financial infrastructure necessary for its upkeep, the new men demonstrated their ability. However, having done so, they began to lose their motivation. The great dynamism and vigour which had been an essential part of the emergent Free Church passed away. Thus the ultimate decline of the Free Church was rooted in the circumstances at its inception, and the social base of its original dynamism.

Social consequences for Aberdeen society. Apart from the bitterness that the Disruption engendered in Aberdeen, the war waged by the Free Church against the Establishment after 1843— although leading to its clear denominational dominance in the city—had important and unforeseen consequences. In the war against the Establishment it seems likely that the first casualties were those working-class members who had seceded and joined the new Church. The emergence of the Free Church run on strict business-like lines with an inquisitorial financial organisation coincided with a period of grave economic recession in the city.[11] The loss of working-class members was never made good by either denomination. Although the evidence suggests a widespread religious commitment among the working class, this commitment never extended to more than intermittent attendance.[12]

The failure of the presbyterian denominations to evangelise the working class was related to events following the Disruption and the great deal of energy and time that went into raising finance for church building and general denominational competition. However, running deeper than this were versions of Calvinist orthodoxy which held that spiritual conversion must necessarily precede any change or improvement in the individual. Thus presbyterian missions tended not to provide facilities related to community development until much later in the century and the emergence of a 'Soup, soap and salvation' approach. In 1846 the Free Church set up eight preaching stations but after one year they were able to claim only four converts. Even these converts were seen in a somewhat doubtful light as a self-evident correlation appeared to exist in the popular mind between prosperity and spiritual election. It followed, therefore, as a logical consequence that the converse also must surely be true. The middle-class dominated church saw economic destitution as being associated with spiritual destitution.

Consequently there was a natural reluctance to accept that those who were so obviously economically destitute could really have undergone a true spiritual conversion. Even the missionary appointed in the South Parish to work among the 'degraded population' had to express doubts about the validity of those who claimed spiritual conversion but remained economically destitute although 'we are bound in all charity to believe that their profession is sincere'.[13] Sin, spiritual destitution, and economic poverty were inextricably bound together.

Ideas such as these haunted Calvinist missionary efforts. They were not new and indeed had a fairly long lineage within Scottish presbyterianism. But in the middle-class dominated Free Church, a narrow orthodoxy combined with a strong financial awareness, seemed to give particular encouragement to such beliefs. However, if the Free Church itself was unable to embrace the spiritually destitute working class, it is clear that it was not prepared to leave such activities to other denominations in the city. A great deal of effort was given over to condemning the doctrinal errors of other, mainly non-presbyterian, denominations.[14] Even the temperance movement was viewed by many ministers with a considerable degree of uncertain opposition, as it was seen as offering secular rather than spiritual intervention as a means of changing individual behaviour.[15] Indeed all social intervention was subjected to a Calvinist theological toothcomb and constrained by the need to present policy within a Calvinist theological framework. Arguably this applied even to action on public health.[16]

The Disruption of the Church of Scotland in 1843 has commonly been portrayed as a triumph of principle over patronage. The popular and remarkable long-lasting image has been of ministers giving up their stipends and their manses, and indeed congregations their churches, and going out to face an uncertain and insecure future. Ultimately the seceders triumph against heavy odds. As far as Aberdeen is concerned such an image is totally misconceived. Indeed in retrospect the balance lay heavily in favour of the seceders, representing as they did the newest and most dynamic elements of the business community. It is unlikely that any seceding minister suffered a reduction in income and although most may have been required to move house, the move may well have been to a more prestigious property. Likewise all congregations were rapidly reinstated either in their former church or in more than comparable buildings closeby. On the other hand, it is clear that some Establishment ministers suffered a loss of stipend. In some cases the drop in income was severe. For example, so impoverished was the Established presbytery following the Disruption that the newly appointed minister of John Knox had no alternative other than to accept whatever the presbytery could afford by way of payment of his stipend.[17] Those remaining in the Church of Scotland were left without ministers; congregations were dispersed as churches were abandoned to the seceders. Communion collections customarily used for distribution to the poor of the parish fell disastrously.

Those who seceded claimed to be creating a church *of* the people. In effect they created within two decades a church *for* the middle class. The Disruption of 1843 was followed by a decade of economic depression and widespread unemployment in the city. The dynamism and energy and time of the seceders was taken up with other things however. In the drive to demonstrate the success of the new Free Church, and thus their own respectability, they put their stamp on a Church which thereafter lost its purpose and direction. And yet perhaps, in their own particular way, they put their stamp on Aberdeen itself. Harriet Beecher Stowe, the American author, was much impressed when she visited the city in the early 1850s and wrote,

> In no city which I visited in Scotland did I see such neatness, order, and thoroughness as in Aberdeen; and in none did there appear to be more gratifying evidence of prosperity and comfort among that class which one sees along the streets and thoroughfares.[18]

Nonetheless at least one important question remains unanswered regarding the Aberdeen clergy and this must now be considered.

James Adam and the Aberdeen clergy. One can see that the social support that the Free Church received made its mark both on church and city; and one can relate this to certain specific features in the city social structure at that time. However, if it is of importance to modify the idea that the Disruption was solely a confrontation over the issue of patronage, it also would be very mistaken to say that principle played no part in the secession. Whilst ministers were encouraged to secede because of the financial promises being offered, this alone does not explain why, unlike any other Scottish city, a complete secession occurred amongst the clergy in Aberdeen. An examination of the backgrounds of the fifteen ministers provides no hint as to why the secession in Aberdeen was so unanimous.[19] Their social origins were typical. They were derived from families whose breadwinners were ministers, farmers, merchants and school-teachers. They were not 'angry young men' but mature middle-aged men born towards the end of the eighteenth and the beginning of the nineteenth century. Neither can one find any leadership pattern by which one or two convinced seceders persuaded the others to follow. Indeed, although all to varying degrees were opposed to patronage in the Church, not all were hardline Evangelicals, and on some social issues they were openly divided. If one can detect any uniformity in the group it was one of fear of loss of respectability. Solace was taken in the fact that secession was unanimous. The Rev. James Foote of the East Parish Church (a man perhaps of more Moderate rather than Evangelical mind) wrote in his diary on his return from the disrupted General Assembly in Edinburgh of the great and undisguised relief he felt that he was not shunned by his friends who continued to receive him very kindly. Because of this 'I was not ashamed to appear on the streets'.[20]

To some extent anxieties such as these can be detected in many other city ministers. Davidson, of the West Parish, declared immediately prior to the Disruption that the next communion he dispensed would be the last in the Establishment but 'not the last he would dispense in the Church of Scotland'. Some claimed that the Free Church was the 'true' Establishment; others that it was God's Establishment.[21] These attitudes however may reveal certain doubts concerning the legitimacy of their actions in seceding but they do not in any way modify the notion of principle involved in that action. Indeed such doubts could be seen as further evidence of the importance of principle in that it acted to over-rule and suppress the fears the ministers genuinely held concerning the loss of respectability which would result as a consequence of secession. This would seem to make their actions all the more laudable.

Therefore a simple explanation for the unanimity of secession in Aberdeen might be the chance coincidence that all fifteen ministers in Aberdeen were motivated by consistently stronger principles than ministers in other Scottish cities. Although this explanation might appear attractive to some observers, it is clear that it lacks plausibility both in terms of statistical probability and, indeed, from an examination of the local evidence. In any case, even if one accepts that principles prevailed, one is left with the need to explain *why* the Aberdeen ministers were so high-minded.

Whilst the backgrounds of the ministers tell us little that appears relevant, and their writings tend to reveal only their lack of resolution on the matter, one has to seek elsewhere an influence which may have been crucial in uniting the actions of these ministers. One has to accept that financial promises must have bolstered principle. However, when one looks for a single unifying influence other than this, it is paradoxical that it emanated from an individual who opposed resolutely the principles on which the seceders stood.

It has been said of James Adam, editor of *Aberdeen Herald*, that 'no other Scottish newspaper allowed less honour to the seceders',[22] and the virulence of Adam's editorial attacks on the Aberdeen clergy more than substantiates such a claim. Adam's dispute with the clergy was a long-standing one. Throughout the 1830s in brilliantly written editorials he combined his advocacy of free trade with a bitter satirical anticlericalism. He appeared particularly to enjoy baiting those who were critical of patronage in the Church of Scotland. No minister in the city had the intellectual ability to confront Adam openly, although at first many were drawn into misguided attempts to do so in the columns of the *Herald*. Some adopted the practice of replying to his 'open letters' in other local newspapers, and were subjected to his ridicule as a consequence.[23] Those who made no response to his editorial comment and would not be drawn into debate received special attention. In such cases Adam would write personally and have his letter delivered to their door to await a reply. Their replies, whether verbal or written, were then printed in full with a commentary.

In 1839 one minister—John Allan of the Union Church—was driven to attack Adam from his pulpit and described him as 'an infidel villain, a blasphemous villain, a hired agent for attacking the clergy, and a satanic agent'. These remarks were reported to James Adam, who then sued Allan for damages. In a long legal battle Adam eventually was awarded £1,000 damages in a case which went to the Court of Session.[24] This, of course, was a very substantial sum at the time and with associated legal costs it probably meant a loss of as much as six years stipend for Allan. The case was important in that it defined boundaries regarding what a minister could say from his pulpit concerning an individual.

Perhaps encouraged by this success, James Adam increased his attacks on the principles of the clergy whose characters were individually and collectively lampooned and ridiculed. Their meetings were described as 'swindle conventicles' — 'the sensible people pity them, the giddy laugh at them, and the weak and the weak only, are gulled by them'. The clergy were described as 'reverend law-breakers', as 'mock martyrs', as 'show martyrs'.[25]

In the heightening tension in the months preceding the Disruption, Adam's venom increased. Each minister was discussed in turn and assessed as to whether when the time came they would follow their strong 'inclination to backslide'. Whilst such assessment would merely have consolidated the intentions of the harder-line Evangelicals, the more Moderate ministers, such as John Murray (North) or James Foote (East), and perhaps even to some extent Alexander Davidson (West), may well have increasingly been confronted by a new fear. The fear of the loss of social respectability after secession was now balanced against the fear of the total loss of 'face' which would be the consequence of remaining in the Establishment.[26] This new fear would be exacerbated by a haunting realisation and recognition of how Adam would depict those who did remain. As if to hammer home this point, in the editorial immediately prior to the Disruption James Adam predicted that few would secede:

They don't go simply *because* they would rather stay. They *pretend* that it would be sinful to remain; but they *know* and *feel* that it must be disagreeable to depart. And the certain discomfort weighs more heavily than the supposed wickedness. They won't go if they can help it.[27]

He was wrong. All fifteen did go. It is somewhat paradoxical that he himself may have played such a central part in consolidating their intentions. James Adam's mistake—one which he recognised after the Disruption—was to underestimate the extent of secession which was to take place in the *laity*. In the event, he wrote bitterly of the seceders who were seeking sympathy when in fact they were enjoying stipends equal to or greater than those who remained in the Establishment.

Finally, although it would be foolish to deny the importance of respect for principle in determining the total secession of the Aberdeen clergy, it would be an oversimplification to see the event solely in these terms. Internal pressures from powerful congregational members, combined with the financial guarantees on offer, eased the decision for many. For those ridiculed in the *Herald* as 'timid schismatics' the intervention of James Adam—a neglected figure in Aberdeen history[28]—may have been crucial.

REFERENCES

1. These occurred in 1733 (Associate Presbytery) and 1752 (Relief Church). The issue of patronage arose in both of these secessions. For an account of these secessions see W. Ferguson, *Scotland, 1689 to the present* (Edinburgh, 1968).
2. R. Rait and G.S. Pryde, *Scotland* (London, 1954), 262.
3. Ibid., 263.
4. For a fuller account see A.A. MacLaren, *Religion and Social Class: The Disruption Years in Aberdeen* (London, 1974), 26-30. The figures are derived from J. McCosh, *The Wheat and the Chaff Gathered into Bundles* (Dundee, 1843).
5. MacLaren, *Religion nd Social Class*, 55-6. The minister who was given a guarantee regarding his snuff was the Rev. Alexander Davidson. See M. Angus, *Sheriff Watson of Aberdeen* (Aberdeen, 1913), 50.
6. The congregation of St Clement's Church set about erecting a temporary wooden building. The Established presbytery was intent on serving an interdict to prevent its erection but tradesmen worked

throughout the night to complete the building before the interdict could
be served. The first sermon was preached in the new building on 4 June
1843. See A. Gammie, *The Churches of Aberdeen* (Aberdeen, 1909), 183.

7. MacLaren, *Religion and Social Class*, 105-6.
8. For a full analysis of the *Census of Religious Worship 1851* and its impli-
    cations for Aberdeen denominations, churches, congregation, and sab-
    bath schools, see Ibid., 31-45.
9. Leader article in *Banner*, 13 May 1843.
10. For biographical details of all the elders in both Established and Free
    churches, see MacLaren, *Religion and Social Class*, 224-55. For a theor-
    etical analysis of the relationship between the eldership and the Aber-
    deen social structure, see A.A. MacLaren, 'Class Formation and Class
    Fractions: The Aberdeen Bourgeoisie 1830-1850' in G. Gordon and B.
    Dicks, *Scottish Urban History* (Aberdeen, 1983), 112-29.
11. In the 1840s Aberdeen textile manufacturing suffered a serious setback
    from which it never recovered with the closure of Leys, Masson & Co.,
    James Hadden & Sons, along with a number of smaller firms. Within
    ten years output had declined from around 81,000 bales to about 9,000.
    The fall in demand for labour was equally dramatic—A. Keith, *The
    North of Scotland Bank Limited* (Aberdeen, 1936), 53-5.
12. Non-attendance need not imply an absence of religious identification
    although it can be seen as a lack of commitment—see Maclaren, *Religion
    and Social Class*, 121-38. The same sort of phenomenon is commented on
    by P.L. Sissons, *The Social Significance of Church Membership in the Burgh of
    Falkirk* (Edinburgh, 1973).
13. Cited in MacLaren, *Religion and Social Class*, chapter 8.
14. Charles Gordon, the local Roman Catholic priest, underwent systematic
    attack for his efforts—James Riddell, *Aberdeen and its Folk* (Aberdeen,
    1868), 79. Money collected for the poor at the Roman Catholic chapel
    was refused by the presbytery—diary entry 27 September 1836, in M.
    Angus, *Sheriff Watson of Aberdeen* (Aberdeen, 1913). Few escaped censure.
    Even a low-profile church such as St John's Episcopal became embroiled
    in a long struggle when they were accused of 'tempting' poor children
    away from the presbyterian school by offering them clothes. Trinity
    Sabbath School Teachers: Minutes of the Quarterly Meeting, 16 Aug.
    1866.
15. Some ministers supported the movement; others saw temperance
    reformers as 'enemies of Christ' who put temperance before the gospel;
    one minister went so far as to claim that 'the devil was the author of the
    Total Abstinence Societies', see A.S. Cook, *Pen Sketches and Reminiscences*
    (Aberdeen, 1901), 4-6, 20-1; J. Bruce, *The Aberdeen Pulpit and Universities*
    (Aberdeen, 1844), 72-3; Scottish Record Office [SRO], CH.2/1/15,
    Records of the Presbytery of Aberdeen, 3 May 1842.
16. A.A. MacLaren, 'Bourgeois ideology and Victorian philanthropy: the

contradictions of cholera' in A.A. MacLaren (ed.), *Social Class in Scotland, Past and Present* (Edinburgh, 1976), 36-54.

17. SRO, Records of the Presbytery of Aberdeen, 3 May 1844. The stipend had been fixed as low as £75 per annum. Similar problems were being faced by Holburn and Gilcomston churches.

18. *Sunny Memories of Foreign Lands* (London, 1854) i, 122.

19. For short biographies of all the city ministers of the Disruption period, see MacLaren, *Religion and Social Class*, 221-4.

20. From the unpublished autobiography of Dr Foote, minister of the East Church in 1843, printed in W. Alexander, *Free East Church Reminiscences* (Aberdeen, 1893), 13.

21. For example, see report in *Aberdeen Herald*, 11 March 1843; *The Banner* (post-Disruption); *Selected Portions of the Diary and Manuscripts of the Rev. Gavin Parker* (Aberdeen, 1848), 1 June 1843: letter from Rev. A.L. Gordon; SRO, Records of the Presbytery of Aberdeen, 28 March 1843.

22. R.M.W. Cowan, *The Newspaper in Scotland* (Glasgow, 1946), 149.

23. See the long series of attacks by Adam in *Aberdeen Herald* throughout January and February 1839, which involved replies and counter-replies. Davidson in desperation wrote to the *Aberdeen Journal* and was ridiculed for doing so. Later Murray and others tried to break off the 'engagement' by doing likewise but failed to escape Adam's attentions.

24. Adam won on a majority verdict. Two judges ruled for Adam; one ruled against. It is typical of James Adam that he did not even bother to comment on the verdict in the *Herald*.

25. *Aberdeen Herald*, 28 Jan., 11 Feb., 4 March 1843.

26. Adam wrote of Davidson that 'he does not seem to have any exalted notion of religious communion—he makes money the climax of its perfection', *Aberdeen Herald*, 11 March 1843. 'Murray and others similarly situated' were more concerned about being 'secure in their livings' than seceding, *ibid.*, 1 April 1843. Foote was treated more leniently and was included no doubt among our 'more weak brethren who will discover strong reasons' for remaining in the Establishment, ibid., 8 April 1843.

27. Ibid., 15 April 1843.

28. It is hoped that James Adam will soon be given the recognition he deserves. An article on his life and times is currently being prepared by the writer for submission to *Northern Scotland*.